YOGA
IN YOUR
SCHOOL

YOGA
IN YOUR SCHOOL

Exercises for Classroom, Gym and Playground

TERESSA ASENCIA

Photographs by Wes Gerrish

PRINCETON BOOK COMPANY, PUBLISHERS

With gratitude to my Yoga teachers,
Baba Muktananda and Gurumayi Chidvilasananda

Text copyright ©2006 by Teressa Asencia
Photographs copyright ©2006 by Wes Gerrish
All rights reserved

Princeton Book Company, Publishers
614 Route 130, Hightstown, NJ 08520
www.princetonbookcompany.com

Although the author has made every effort to ensure that the poses presented in this book are safe, please practice only the poses that are comfortable for you and your students. The author, publisher, participants and distributors of this book disclaim any liability in connection with the exercises and advice herein.

Library of Congress Cataloging-in-Publication Data

Asencia, Teressa.
    Yoga in your school: excercises for classroom, gym, and playground / Teressa Asencia.
        p. cm.
    Includes bibliographical references (p.   ).
    ISBN 0-87127-286-5
    1. Hatha yoga for children. 2. Exercise for children. I. Title.

RJ133.7.A84 2006
613.7'046083-dc22

2006046004

Cover and interior design by John McMenamin

6   5   4   3   2   1

Also in the School Physical Activity Series:
Dancing In Your School by Anne Dunkin

Printed in Canada

To Celeste and Orson

The secret of a better world

lives in the hearts of our children.

CONTENTS

Introduction: Take a Yoga Break x

One • Why Yoga in Your School? 1

Integrate Yoga Breaks into Your Daily Schedule 3

Why Take a Yoga Break? 3

When to Take a Yoga Break 4

Where to Take a Yoga Break 4

The Breath 4

"Breathing Breaks" for the classroom 5

Coordinating breath with movement 5

Dynamic Postures 6

Static Postures 6

Two • Energy/Enthusiasm 8

Start the Day with Stretching 8

The Pyramid 9

Cactus Twist 10

Side Stretch 11

Forward Bend 12

Jumping Frog 13

Relaxing Body and Mind 14

Elbow Circles 14

Seated Spinal Twist 15

Easy Triangle Pose 17

Eye Exercises 18

"See the Best" Contemplation 19

When Energy and Attention Wane 20

Chaise Longue 20

Chaise Longue Contemplation 20

The Flying Dolphin 21

Golden Gate Bridge 22

Bicycle Built for Two 23

Energizing Breath 24

Three • Strength/Courage 25

  Inner and Outer Strength 25

    The Cat Pose 26

    The Stretching Cat 27

    Downward Dog Pose 27

    Triangle 28

    Twisting Triangle 29

  Practicing Patience and Perseverance 30

    Side Stretch at Desk 30

    Half Moon 31

    Double Silent Tree 33

    Warrior 34

    Double Warrior 35

  Open the Window to Insight, Intuition and Inner Wisdom 36

    Intense Forward Stretch 36

    The Space between Each Breath 38

    Upside Down 38

    The Space between the Eyebrows Breathing Technique 39

Four • Concentration/Balance 40

  Enhancing Concentration 40

    Nataraja 40

    The Tree 41

    The Eagle 42

    Double Boat 43

    Golden Channel Breathing Technique 43

  Experiencing the present moment 44

    Arm Stretch at Desk 44

    Penguin Stretch 45

    Hair-Raising Stretch 46

    The Boat 47

    Be the Witness Breathing Technique 48

  Balancing Activity with Quiet Time 49

    The Bridge 50

    Lunge 50

    Waterfall 51

    The Grape Press 52

    Open the Window Breathing Technique 52

Five • Harmony/Friendship 54

  Building Trust and Friendship 55

    Circle of Friendship 55

    Circle of Friendship Game 56

    Two Frogs on a Lotus 56

    The Toboggan 57

    Twin Triangle 58

  The Circle of Giving and Receiving 59

    Friendship Chair 59

    Forward Backbend 59

    Sailboat Stretch 60

    Twin Spinal Twist 61

    Standing Back-to-Back Twist 62

    The Moving Pillow Breathing Technique 62

  Creating a Harmonious Classroom 63

    Stretch Up 63

    Seated Forward Bend 64

    Cobbler's Stretch 65

    Back to Back Breathing Technique 65

    Pink Cloud Contemplation 66

Six • Joy/Contentment 67

  Bursting with Joy 69

    Bursting into Blossom 69

    Growing Sunflower 69

    Double Dancers 70

    Tango Twist 70

  Creativity Flows From a Quiet Mind 72

    Sun-Moon Breath 72

    Cloudless Sky Contemplation 73

  Cultivating Contentment 73

    Butterfly 73

    The Laughing Table 74

    Soothing Stretch 75

    Cultivating Contentment Breathing Technique 75

    Contentment Contemplation 77

Seven • Silence/Stillness 78

    Preparing for Exams 79

        Blade Squeeze 79

        Touching the Stars 80

        Clearing the Mind Breathing Technique 81

        Brain Stimulating Forward Bend 82

        Three-Part Breath 83

    Sinking into Silence 84

        Split Lunge 84

        Sinking into Silence 85

        The Calm Blue Lake Breathing Technique 86

        The Blue Balloon Breathing Technique 87

        The Sound of Silence Contemplation 88

    End the Day Together in Stillness 89

        Silent Stretch 89

        Standing Dolphin 90

        Spinal Breath Breathing Technique 90

        End of the Day Contemplation 91

References and Resources 93

AUTHOR'S NOTE

Perhaps the seeds for this book were planted inside me at an early age. At age four when I did not want to leave the playground to come inside for lunch when called, I was put in a room alone and then expelled from nursery school. When it was time to enter first grade, my mother carried me kicking and screaming to the door of the school. As I sat inside my stuffy classroom for the next few years, my body often felt tense and yearned to move as I eagerly counted the long minutes before each short recess.

One of my first memories of effective learning took place when my eighth grade teacher gave us an extra-curricular course on listening skills. Another striking experience of effective learning took place at the Writers' Workshop at the University of Iowa when a well-known poet taught my class how good writing is perfectly simple and always written from personal experience.

May the simple style of this book be an ode to his "mantra", "The fewer the words, the more the meaning." May my thirty years of personal experience with the simple, powerful and delicious techniques presented in this book, jump off the pages and inspire teachers and students to share a more enjoyable, effective learning process.

INTRODUCTION

Take a Yoga Break

*"Simplicity is the most difficult thing to secure in this world.
It is the last limit of experience and the last effort of genius."*
George Sand

What is Yoga?

Yoga is an ancient science that originated in India 5000 years ago. In simple terms, Yoga teaches the art of living a healthy and happy life. The Sanskrit word "Yoga" means yoke or "union." The essence of Yoga is the experience of the unity inherent in all creation.

The form of Yoga that has recently become popular in the Western world is Hatha Yoga, which consists of a series of comprehensive physical exercises and breathing techniques designed to rejuvenate every part of the body and calm the mind. While strengthening both body and mind, these exercises also tone the muscles, expand breathing capacity, soothe the nervous system and energize and harmonize body and mind. Some exercises also enhance concentration, inspire moral courage, and teach qualities such as patience and insight.

After thirty years of study, research and teaching in Yoga, the author has extracted the essential elements and adapted these techniques into simple exercises that can easily be taught in the modern classroom to enhance the learning process.

The techniques presented in Yoga in Your School are ideal for use in regular classrooms, playgrounds and physical education classes in schools. Many of the exercises in this book may also be used in camps, community and recreation centers, and also in dance and yoga classes for children.

ONE

Why Yoga in Your School?

"I am convinced that work is love in action.
If we thought like this, we would do great things."
Jean Pinchert Dixon

Teaching is one of the most essential professions and also one of the most demanding. This book is designed to give teachers simple techniques to enhance their own energy as they inspire students to enjoy a more efficient and joyous learning process.

Being a successful teacher requires great energy, inner strength, resourcefulness and creativity. As with any classroom instruction, it is important for the teacher to provide the model. If teachers have inner strength and harmony, children will feel it and imbibe it. Through sharing the simple techniques presented in this book, teachers may inspire students to enhance both physical and mental strength and develop habits that will enable them to take responsibility for their own well-being for the rest of their lives.

Children love to move. In the traditional classroom, children are very sedentary. When they sit still too long, they feel tense and it is more difficult for them to learn. With a few movement and breathing exercises daily, teachers may easily release this tension and inspire students to tap into their innate wisdom, creativity and potential.

Most of the exercises may be practiced in a small space such as a regular class-room. Many of the breathing exercises and simple movement exercises may be done while sitting at a desk or standing beside a desk. Other exercises are ideal for larger spaces such as the gymnasium, playground or sports field. Teachers are encouraged to adapt these exercises for their particular circumstances.

The Benefits of *Yoga in Your School*

"Within the next five to ten years, Yoga in school will be the norm."

Mariam Gates,
Child Magazine,
September 2003

Our modern world is highly advanced in technology, yet we have lost many of the ancient keys to the knowledge of the art of living. Recently, Yoga has become increasingly popular worldwide and an estimated 35 million people in North America now take a Yoga class once a week.

Yoga is currently practiced in many educational institutions worldwide. In France, South America, India, Italy and several other European countries, Yoga has been taught in schools for more than twenty-five years. Many schools in North America have already trained teachers to include Yoga as a regular part of the class-room day. It is also becoming more common as a regular part of the physical educa-tion curriculum where it offers a non-competitive alternative to competitive sports.

It is possible to build body strength and flexibility through many forms of physical exercise. The unique aspect of Yoga is that it builds both inner and outer strength, endurance and flexibility. In addition to enhancing physical and mental well-being, Yoga teaches students to concentrate, releases tension and develops inner qualities such as patience and insight. With regular practice, students learn to devel-op better self-control, inner confidence and focus. Regular Yoga practice unifies the two sides of the brain, allowing information and knowledge to enter the brain at deeper levels. Practicing the exercises together enhances the relationship between teacher and students, enabling them to work together productively and enjoy the learning process.

Integrate Yoga Breaks into Your Daily Schedule

Yoga in Your School presents a series of short "Yoga breaks," simple breathing and movement exercises that teachers may easily insert into their daily classroom schedule. Each exercise takes less than three minutes, so that teachers may present them regularly or as needed, when attention or energy begins to wane. These short exercise segments may also be combined creatively to create longer sequences for physical education classes, playgrounds, athletics, recreation centers, camps, and dance schools. Taking a few minutes to breathe and stretch between activities will allow students to better assimilate knowledge learned, create a more harmonious classroom and inspire a more joyful, effective learning process.

"What lies behind us and what lies before us are tiny matters compared to what lies within us."

Ralph Waldo Emerson

Why Take a Yoga Break?

- Develop motor skills and balance

- Create physical and mental strength and flexibility

- Energize body and mind and bring more oxygen to the blood cells and brain

- Make breath, blood and lymph fluids circulate better

- Release physical and mental tensions that have accumulated while students have been sitting for a long time

- Enhance concentration

- Develop better listening skills

- Improve posture

- Bring students into the present moment

- Exercise the body and balance the emotions

- Open the shoulders and chest, allowing students to relax and breathe deeper during their classes

- Open the hip joints and prepare students to sit comfortably

- Teach patience and insight

- Create a calm harmonious classroom

When to Take a Yoga Break

- First thing in the morning
- During classes when energy or attention begins to wane
- Between activities
- While students are waiting in line
- Before and after lunch
- After recess
- Before examinations
- When students are tense, tired or restless
- At the end of the day

Where to Take a Yoga Break

- Classroom
- Physical education class or gymnasium
- Playground
- School courtyard
- Athletic field
- Recreation center
- Camp
- Dance or Yoga studio

The Breath

Breath is a sacred word in every culture. In Sanskrit it is called "prana" or life force. In Chinese it is "Chi," vital force or energy. To the African Bushman it is "Kung," or life. The breath is a great source of energy and has the power to release physical, mental and emotional tension.

"Breathing Breaks" for the classroom

Breathing exercises are ideal for the classroom as they are easy to learn and can be practiced while sitting at a desk. Some of these techniques are energizing, while others have a calming or harmonizing effect. You may insert "Breathing Breaks" into your daily routine several times a day. Breathing exercises are especially useful when students are overactive, tired or stressed. Some breathing exercises may be most useful for specific situations like preparing for exams or when returning to the classroom after recess or lunch to regain concentration. You may use your own creativity and resourcefulness to adapt these techniques to suit the particular needs of your students.

Coordinating the breath with movement

Always give instructions for each physical movement in coordination with the breath. For example, before raising the arms above the head, you would tell your students to "inhale and raise your arms up, and place your hands on your head with one hand resting on top of the other." Before lowering the arms, you would say, "exhale slowly as you lower the arms." Always give the breathing instruction before the movement instruction.

Remind your students to concentrate on the breath in coordination with each physical movement and to let the breath become slower and more subtle with each exhalation. The secret of Yoga is to concentrate completely on the breath and use the breath to release the body more with each exhalation.

The breath is always longer than the movement

The Breath   1 _____ 6

The Movement   2 _____ 5

Since each breath is longer than each movement, always begin the breath before the movement. For example, for a movement count of six, you would instruct your students to inhale on one and begin the movement on two and continue moving on count three, four, and five. Although the movement is complete on count five, instruct your students to continue inhaling to count six. Then, you would instruct them to begin their exhale on count one and begin moving on count two and continue moving on count three, four, and five. After the movement is complete on count five, instruct your students to continue to exhale during count six.

Generally, the inhalation and exhalation are the same number of counts. To create a more energizing effect, make each inhalation longer than each exhalation. To create a more calming, relaxing effect, make each exhalation longer than each inhalation.

Remember to breathe

Sometimes students are so focused on doing the movement correctly, that they forget to breathe. If you notice that your students have tension in their bodies or have facial expressions that indicate they are not breathing deeply, gently remind them to breathe by saying "remember to breathe" or "breathe with each movement."

Dynamic Postures

By repeating a simple movement several times, or using a series of variations, you may encourage students to gently release deeper into the stretch with each exhalation. Talk your students through each movement by coordinating it with the breath. Tell them to "feel the body stretch or lengthen with each inhalation" and to "let the body soften and release more into the pose with each exhalation."

Static Postures

After they have repeated the same movement a few times in coordination with the breath, encourage students to concentrate on the breath while holding a particular Yoga pose. By holding the movement for several breaths, students learn patience and concentration.

Concentrating on the breath as it becomes slower and more subtle with each exhalation allows them to effortlessly release more into the stretch with each exhalation. As they rest in the pose, tell them to "feel the breath stretch or lengthen the body with each inhalation." With each exhalation, tell your students to "let the breath become slower and more subtle." As they rest in the pose concentrating on the breath, remind them to "feel the body soften and release more into the pose with each exhalation."

Many of the poses in this book are presented in both dynamic and static versions. Generally, begin with the dynamic version, then practice the static version.

Remind your students to:

- Breathe deeply and coordinate each movement with their breathing
- Remember to respect their unique bodies and never strain
- Concentrate on the breath and turn within rather than compare themselves with other classmates
- Imagine their body is lengthening from inside on each inhalation
- Feel their body release more into the pose with each exhalation

Teachers, remind yourselves that:

- You may also benefit from doing the exercises with your students
- You may take a private Yoga Break at home after school to dissolve stress and rejuvenate your body, mind and spirit
- You may be resourceful and creative in adapting these exercises to the needs of your students. For example, if one of your students has a physical impairment you may use a modified or alternative exercise.

"Ahhhh…, it's time for a "Yoga Break!"

T W O

Energy/Enthusiasm

*"Enthusiasm is the greatest power. For one endowed with enthusiasm,
nothing is impossible in this world."*

Ramayana

Start the Day with Stretching

This series of simple stretching exercises teaches how to
coordinate the breath with movement. By practicing
them, students learn how the body, mind and breath work
together for maximum benefit. A few short Yoga breaks
during the day teach students how to take charge of their
own mental and physical well-being.

Many of the exercises presented in this chapter may be practiced while sitting
at a desk or standing next to a desk. Teachers may also encourage students to bring
a carpet, mat or towel to create their own exercise space.

Awaken powerful forces lying dormant inside the body

In the morning, the body is often stiff and needs to be stretched, but the mind is
fresh and easily focused. Morning is an ideal time to train the mind to concentrate
and turn within to discover the joy and well-being that will that will enable you to
enjoy a calm, centered state all day. Start the day together with a series of stretching
postures and progress into a vigorous warm-up that awakens every part of the body.

Enhancing Harmony in the Classroom

Simply by concentrating on the breath and doing the same simple movement
exercise together, your class may experience the harmony and union that is the
essence of Yoga.

The Pyramid

Sit in a chair with your feet flat on the floor. Inhaling, raise your arms to the sides and up over your head, bringing the palms of your hands together above your head.

Dynamic version

Exhale and press your palms together as you bend toward the right. Inhale and expand back to center. Repeat this movement ten times to the right side, coordinating each movement with the breath. Feel how this movement stretches the left side of the body and strengthens all the muscles in the arms.

Continue to coordinate the breath with each movement as you repeat this ten times to the other side. Let each exhalation be long and slow. After the tenth exhalation, return to center.

Static version

Repeat the pyramid pose and hold the stretch to each side for three breaths. With each inhalation, press your palms together and feel the spine lengthen as the chest and rib cage expand. With each exhalation, feel your body naturally releasing further into the stretch.

When you are ready to release the pose, inhale as you return to center. Exhaling, slowly release the arms to the sides.

Benefits of the *Pyramid*:

The *Pyramid* creates expansion in the shoulders and chest, stretches the sides of the body and strengthens the arms. It is a good pose to practice after students have been sitting at their desks, reading or writing for some time. By coordinating the breath with each movement, students learn to concentrate on the breath and use it to release the body more with each exhalation.

Cactus Twist

Inhale and raise your arms with your elbows bent at shoulder level.

Dynamic version

Exhale slowly as you twist to the left side, placing your right hand on your left shoulder.

Inhale deeply as you return to center. Exhale and twist to the right side bringing your right hand to rest on your left shoulder. Inhale again as you return to center. You may repeat this pose several times to each side, coordinating each movement with the breath.

Static version

Exhale and twist to the left side. Inhale deeply and concentrate on the breath as you rest in the twist position for three deep breaths. With each exhalation, let your breath become slower and more subtle and feel your body easily twisting more to the left. After the third long exhalation, inhale deeply as you return to center. Exhale slowly as you twist to the right side. Inhale deeply and concentrate on the breath as you rest in the twist position for three deep breaths. With each exhalation, let your breath become slower and more subtle and feel your body easily twisting more to the left. After the third long exhalation, inhale deeply as you return to center.

Benefits of the *Cactus Twist*

The simple twist teaches how to coordinate the breath with the movement and enhances concentration. The twisting movement stimulates thousands of nerve endings in the spine. It is a good pose to practice after sitting for some time and helps release tension in the back, shoulders and neck.

Side Stretch

Dynamic version

Stand with your feet parallel and your arms at your sides. Inhale and raise your left arm up with your elbow resting alongside your ear as your fingertips stretch toward the ceiling. Exhale slowly and bend toward your right side. Inhale deeply and return to center. Exhale slowly as you lower your arm.

Inhaling, raise your right arm up with your elbow resting alongside your ear as your fingertips stretch toward the ceiling. Exhaling slowly, bend toward the left side.

Inhale and return to center. Exhale slowly as you lower your arm.

Continue to concentrate on the breath and coordinate it with each movement as you repeat the dynamic version of this stretch several times to each side.

11

Static version

Hold the stretch to each side for three breaths. Inhaling, feel your arm and your entire side lengthen upward. Exhaling, feel your body release more into the stretch. On the next inhalation, feel the increased extension on your stretched side and down into your foot as you press your foot on the floor and stretch up through your arm.

When you are ready to release the pose, inhale as you return to center. Exhaling, slowly release your arm down.

Benefits of the *Side Stretch*:

This stretch lengthens the side of the body and expands the rib cage, increasing lung capacity. It is a good pose to practice after students have been sitting for some time.

Forward Bend

1. Stand with your feet parallel. Inhale and raise your arms up alongside your ears.

2. Feel the breath elongate your spine. Exhaling slowly, fall forward, bringing your head toward your knees. If it is comfortable, touch the floor with your fingertips or the palms of your hands.

1.

Concentrate completely on the breath as you rest in this position for three deep inhalations and exhalations. With each exhalation let the breath be softer and more subtle as you release your torso further with each breath. Feel how the dynamic lift of the legs allows for a passive release of the torso.

On the next inhalation, slowly return to center. Close your eyes and rest here for a few moments, observing the breath and the effects of the pose.

2.

Easy version of the *Forward Bend*

If you are not yet flexible enough to bend forward with your legs straight, bend your knees and place your elbows on your knees as you rest in this pose.

On the next inhalation, slowly return to center. Close your eyes and rest here for a few moments, observing the breath and the effects of the pose.

Benefits of the *Forward Bend:*

The increased supply of blood to the upper body revitalizes the nerve endings in the spinal column. In addition to stretching the hamstrings and strengthening the legs, this pose also tones the internal organs, releases the spine, nourishes the brain and calms the mind.

Jumping Frog

Dynamic version

Inhaling, open your arms diagonally back and look up as you feel your chest expand with breath.

Exhale slowly as you bend your knees and bend forward into a squat. Relax your head forward as you stretch your arms in front and bring your fingertips together near the floor.

Inhale and expand back up to a standing position as you open your arms to the diagonal back and look up. Repeat this three times, coordinating each movement with the breath.

Static version

On the next exhalation, bend forward and rest in a squat for three breaths. With each inhalation, breathe in deeply and feel your upper body expand. Let each exhalation become slower and softer. Feel how your body effortlessly releases more with each breath.

On the next inhalation, slowly return to a standing position. Close your eyes and rest here for a few moments experiencing the effects of this pose.

Benefits of the *Jumping Frog*:

The *Jumping Frog* opens the chest, increases lung capacity and releases tension in the neck and shoulders. It is a good pose to get energy moving after students have been sitting for a long time.

Relaxing Body and Mind

Tension drains vitality. It is important to take time every day for rest and restorative activities to release the stress that accumulates in the body and mind. This series of soothing poses relieves stress, allowing the natural vital force to flow through the body and mind undiminished.

Elbow Circles

Inhaling, raise your arms to shoulder level and stretch your arms out to the side with the palms facing up. Exhaling, raise your palms up and bend your elbows to touch your shoulders with your fingers.

Inhale and rotate your elbows forward and up. Exhaling, continue to roll your shoulders to the back and down. Continue to coordinate the breath with each movement as you move your elbows around in small circles. Gradually, make the circles bigger and bigger until the tips of the elbows touch in front.

Now, reverse the direction, inhaling up and back and exhaling down and to the front. Concentrate on the breath as you begin with small circles and gradually make the circles bigger and bigger.

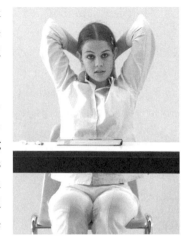

Bring your arms back to center, still bent. Then move your arms backward and forward. Inhaling, stretch your arms back. Exhale and bring your arms forward. Try to touch your elbows together in front on each inhalation. With each exhalation let any tension in your neck and shoulders go out with the breath. Continue like this for three deep breaths.

Now move your shoulders and elbows up and down. Inhaling, stretch your elbows up and try to touch the backs of your hands together behind your neck. Exhaling, bring your shoulders and elbows down, touching your waist with your elbows. Continue at your own rhythm. As you move, lift your neck and head keeping them in line with the spine. Continue a few times, letting go of any residue of tension in your neck, shoulders and upper back. On the next inhalation, bring your arms to shoulder level. Exhaling, turn your palms down and lower your arms.

Benefits of *Elbow Circles:*

This movement releases tension in the neck, shoulders and upper back muscles. It is a good pose to practice after sitting for some time.

Seated Spinal Twist

Sit in a chair with your feet flat on the floor. Inhale and feel the breath expand down your spine.

Dynamic version

Exhaling, turn toward the right and place your left hand on your right knee. Continue to exhale slowly and press your right knee toward the left with your left hand as you twist toward the right side. Stretch your right hand behind your back and look toward the right with your head and eyes.

Inhaling, continue to elongate your spinal column as you return to center front. Exhale and turn toward your left, placing your right hand on your left knee. Press your knee toward the left as your right hand stretches around your body. Look all the way to the left with your head and eyes. On the inhalation, slowly release your hands and return to center front.

Static version

Repeat the spinal twist and hold the twist for three breaths. On the inhalation, lengthen your spinal column. Exhaling, turn toward your right and place your left hand on your right knee. Continue to exhale slowly and press your right knee toward the left with your left hand as you

twist toward your right side. Stretch your right hand behind your back and look toward your right with your head and eyes. Rest here and breathe in deeply. Visualize the breath expanding down your spinal column. Hold the breath in for a moment and concentrate on your coccyx. Exhaling, visualize the breath expanding back up through each vertebra. On the next inhalation, feel the breath expanding your rib cage. Now, as you exhale long and slowly, relax the muscles in your back and gently twist a little more. Rest here for another deep breath. Visualize the breath expanding down your spinal column on the inhalation and lengthening up through each vertebra on the exhalation. On the next inhalation, return to center and repeat the twist to the left side.

Benefits of the *Seated Spinal Twist*:

This pose releases all the muscles in the back that have been in a static position from sitting at a desk for long periods of time. The twisting movement also tones the spinal nerves, massages the abdominal organs, relieves tension in the neck and has a relaxing effect on the nervous system.

Easy Triangle Pose

1. Stand with your feet in a wide stance. Your feet should be as wide apart as the length of one of your legs. Inhale and open your arms to the sides. Breathe in deeply, expanding your chest with breath. Press your thigh muscles against the bone, so your legs are very strong.

1.

2. Turn your left foot to the left 90 degrees and your right foot toward the left about 30 degrees. Make sure that the heel of your left foot is in line with the arch of your right foot and keep both hips facing front.

3. Exhale and wrap your right arm around your back to keep your hips facing front. Bend your left leg, bringing your left forearm to rest just above your left knee. Keep your left knee directly over your left ankle. Ideally, your left thigh is parallel to the floor. If this is difficult, try bringing your legs wider apart. Turn your head to look up and rest here for three breaths.

2.

With each inhalation, feel the breath expand your body in all directions. With each exhalation, relax more into the pose. When you have completed three deep breaths, inhale as you slowly return to center. Release your legs and shake out any tension, then repeat this pose to the other side.

3.

Benefits of the *Easy Triangle*:

This pose opens the shoulders, increases lung capacity and strengthens the legs as it quiets the body and calms the mind. It also stretches the spine and opens the hips. It is the easiest version of the Triangle pose and prepares the body for the more advanced versions.

Variation: *Extended Triangle*

With each inhalation, breathe in deeply and stretch your left arm up alongside your ear. Rest here with your body still as a mountain and your breath flowing like a river. With each exhalation, turn your chest more toward the left and pull your shoulders back and down. With each inhalation, stretch up through your arm and feel the wonderful stretch all the way down your side. As you exhale, slowly sink deeper into an inner stillness.

Benefits of the *Extended Triangle*:

The *Extended Triangle* increases flexibility in the legs, hips and back. It also stretches the spine and opens the shoulder joints and brings the body and mind into balance.

Eye Exercises

Our eyes work all the time. Take a moment to think of all the things the eyes help you with. Perhaps the eyes would also appreciate a little break.

Sit in your chair in a comfortable position with your feet flat on the floor. Moving only the muscles of your eyes, look all the way up. Slowly move your eyes in the clockwise direction, stretching them as far as possible. Move your eyes past 1 o'clock, 2, 3, 4, 5, 6 o'clock, 7, 8, 9, 10, 11 and up to 12 o'clock.

Now reverse the direction. Again, look all the way up to 12 o'clock. Now move your eyes in a counterclockwise direction. Feel the stretch deep in the muscles of your eyes as they move in the opposite direction past, 11 o'clock, 10, 9, 8, 7, 6 o'clock, 5, 4, 3, 2, 1, and back up to 12 o'clock.

Now close your eyes and rub the palms of your hands together to create heat. Inhale deeply and place your warm palms over your eyes.

Feel the muscles deep in your eyes absorb the heat. Exhale slowly and bring your head to rest on your desk.

As you rest here, take a moment to thank your eyes for all the things they allow you to see and do every day.

Benefits of the Eye Exercises:

This is a simple yet very effective exercise that you may do anytime you feel tiredness or strain in the eyes.

"See the Best" Contemplation

Practice seeing the best qualities in your students, teachers and friends. Close your eyes for a few moments and see one of the best qualities of someone in your class.

Chaise Longue

Partner One, sit with your legs extended in front of you. Partner Two, lie down on your back with your hips touching your partner's lower back and the backs of your legs resting against his upper back and head.

Breathe in deeply and feel how the breath expands your torso and allows your legs and feet to lengthen. As you exhale, let all your muscles soften and feel yourself sinking deeper into the floor. Rest here as long as you like, then change positions with your partner and repeat this pose.

Benefits of the *Chaise Longue*:

The *Chaise Longue* gives a rest to the heart and drains the lymph glands in the legs. This inverted position takes the weight off the legs, bringing an increased supply of blood to the upper body. This restful pose rejuvenates both body and mind and creates a feeling of serenity.

Chaise Longue Contemplation

As you rest in this pose, close your eyes and imagine a beautiful pink cloud. Put your thoughts or worries on this cloud and watch them float away.

When Energy and Attention Wane

When students are tired or restless, try the poses in this section to improve concentration, increase circulation and enhance energy.

The Flying Dolphin

Sit on the edge of your chair and place your feet flat on the floor about two and a half feet apart. Inhale and feel the breath expand your rib cage. Breathe out long and lean forward, placing your elbows on your inner thighs. As you breathe in deeply, gently press your inner thighs with your elbows and feel the breath go all the way down into the outside of your feet.

On the next exhalation, fall forward bringing your head toward your knees. Inhaling, cross your arms, placing your hands on the opposite elbows. Rest here for three deep breaths.

On the next inhalation, stretch your arms forward and place the palms of your hands on the floor. Exhaling, walk your hands forward on the floor as far as is comfortable. Rest here for a few moments and, with each inhalation, visualize the breath expanding your lower back and lengthening your spine. With each exhalation, let the breath become softer.

On the next inhalation, lift your arms up behind your back until your torso and head lift up like a flying dolphin. Exhaling, fall forward again. Continue for three deep breaths, lifting your arms and torso up with each inhalation and releasing forward with each exhalation.

When you have completed three deep inhalations and exhalations, inhale slowly and return to a seated position. Close your eyes and rest here a few moments.

Benefits of the *Flying Dolphin*:

This pose gives a deep stretch to the muscles of the neck and shoulders. It also stretches the spinal column and enhances circulation in the upper body. Since this exercise increases energy in the upper body and clears the mind, it is recommended when students seem distracted or restless.

Golden Gate Bridge

Stand facing your partner. Grasp your partner's hands and walk away from each other. Exhaling, bend at the hips and take a few more little steps back until your arms and back are in a straight line. Keep your legs straight and your heels on the floor. Inhaling, stretch your sit bones back, away from your partner.

Feel your spine expanding and your shoulder joints opening. Exhaling, allow your full weight to extend away from your partner. Inhale deeply, breathing into the base of your spine. Exhale long, letting the muscles around your shoulders soften and release further. Again, breathe in deeply. Enjoy the opening around your shoulder blades. Exhale long as you rest here a few more moments.

When you are ready to release the pose, take a few steps toward your partner, release your hands and slowly roll up.

Benefits of the *Golden Gate Bridge*:

This deep partner stretch produces a unique release in the entire shoulder girdle. The polarity created by pulling against your partner expands the spine and creates a powerful opening in the shoulder joints, releasing tension in the shoulders and back. It also strengthens the legs and develops trust. It is a good pose to release tension in the back, neck and shoulders after sitting for a long time.

Bicycle Built for Two

Lie on your back with your knees bent and the soles of your feet touching your partner's feet. Inhale and exhale in coordination with each movement of your legs. Push against your partner's feet and begin to peddle your bicycle up a big hill.

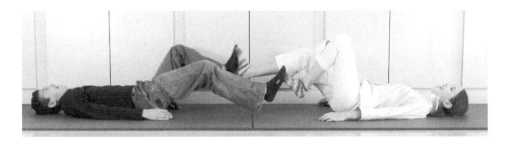

Breathe in deep and breathe out long as you synchronize your movements and breathing with your partner.

Once you reach the top of the hill, let your breath become slower and softer as you gently push your feet against your partner's and peddle faster and faster down the hill. Experiment with different speeds, synchronizing each movement with the breath.

When you are ready, release your feet away from your partner's, bend your knees and place the soles of your feet on the floor. Close your eyes and rest here for a few moments, observing your breath.

Benefits of the *Bicycle Built for Two*:

This simple and fun partner pose enhances circulation in the legs and releases mental and physical tension. It is a great pose to practice whenever students are restless, tired or stressed. Sometimes, a short *Bicycle Built for Two* break that inspires students to let off steam and laugh for a few moments also does wonders to enhance their ability to concentrate on the next academic activity.

Energizing Breath

Sit in a comfortable position with your spine elongated. Close your eyes.

Inhale fully, expanding the abdomen completely with breath. Exhale and contract the abdomen to forcefully expel the air through the nostrils. Inhale again, letting the breath expand the abdomen. Exhaling, contract the abdomen and release the breath.

Continue like this for ten breaths. The exhalation should be forceful and audible. Repeat the energizing breath again ten times at your own rhythm. When you have completed ten fast and forceful breaths, let your breath return to normal. Rest here a few moments observing the breath as it returns to normal.

Benefits of the *Energizing Breath*:

This dynamic breathing technique tones the nervous system and clears the mind. It is an effective exercise to practice anytime to increase energy and alertness.

THREE

Strength / Courage

"Courage is nothing less than the force to surmount danger, evil, fear and injustice while continuing to affirm that life is beautiful and good…and that tomorrow is another day."
Dorothy Thompson

The unique aspect of Yoga is that it builds outer strength, endurance and flexibility as it also develops inner strengths such as courage, patience and insight. While toning the body and focusing the mind, Yoga practice also strengthens the nervous system and helps students to better manage the tensions of daily life.

Inner and Outer Strength

This series of Yoga poses is designed to build both inner and outer strength and create a strong, flexible body and mind. This dynamic routine includes a series of poses that increase circulation, enhance endurance, strengthen the legs and create a powerful, alert mind.

25

The Cat Pose

"One's own thought is one's world. What a person thinks is what he becomes."

Maitri Upanishad

Come up on all fours and place the hands slightly in front of the shoulders. Inhaling, lift the head and the base of the spine toward the ceiling. Look up and visualize your breath expanding down your spinal column. Hold the breath for a moment and concentrate on the coccyx.

Exhale slowly as you drop your head, press your hands on the floor and lift the small of the back toward the ceiling

Repeat the cat arch, coordinating the breath with each movement for three deep inhalations and exhalations.

Inhale and drop your spine in its natural curve again, with your head and coccyx lifting toward the ceiling. Exhaling, arch your back and release your head and neck completely. Inhaling, drop your spine into a curve again and observe your breath expanding down your spinal column. Hold the breath for a moment and concentrate on your coccyx. Exhaling, press on your hands and soften your rib cage as you arch your back a bit higher. Repeat this pose, concentrating completely on the breath.

Benefits of the *Cat Pose*:

The *Cat Pose* strengthens the back and reduces tension in the back and shoulders. The arching movement stretches the lower back, massages the spine, strengthens the arms and allows the chest and lungs to expand.

The Stretching Cat

Come up on your hands and knees. Inhale and lift your left leg.

Exhaling, bend your left leg, bringing the knee toward your head. Relax your shoulders and drop your head toward your knee. As you inhale, lift your left leg up in back again. Repeat this pose for three deep breaths. Then repeat this pose with the right leg for three breaths.

On the third exhalation, release your left leg, sit back on your heels and bring your forehead to the floor. Rest here for a few moments in the child's pose.

Benefits of *Cat Pose* with leg lift:

This version of the cat pose stretches the entire front of the body, and strengthens the arms and legs. It creates a strong flexible spine and warms up the body to prepare for the more advanced poses.

Downward Dog Pose

Start on your hands and knees with your palms down on the floor, directly under your shoulders. Exhaling, curl your toes under and press on your hands to straighten your legs and lift your hips. Rest here for three deep breaths.

With each inhalation, stretch your coccyx toward the sky and your head toward the floor. With each exhalation, gently press your palms on the floor and feel your spine elongate as you lift your kneecaps and press your heels toward the floor. Feel the stretch in your hamstring muscles. Again, breathe in deeply, elongating the spine. Breathe out slowly, lifting the coccyx more. Inhaling, widen the shoulders and lengthen the neck. Exhaling, relax the base of the throat.

When you are ready to release this pose, exhale as you come back to all fours. Then sit back to rest on your heels, close your eyes and observe your breath for a few moments.

Benefits of the *Downward Dog* pose:

This pose strengthens the legs, opens the shoulder joints and stretches the spine and the hamstrings. This is a recommended warm-up for gym class and athletics. It enhances blood circulation, dissolves fatigue and restores energy.

Triangle

Stand with your feet in a wide stance. Your feet should be as wide apart as the length of one of your legs. Inhale and open your arms to the sides. Breathe in deeply, expanding your chest with breath.

Turn your left foot to your left 90 degrees and your right foot toward the left about 30 degrees. Place the heel of your left foot in line with the arch of your right

foot and keep both hips facing front. (Photos depicting the above instructions for the two start-up poses for the *Triangle* are shown in the *Easy Triangle* on page 17.)

Then exhale slowly and stretch to your left side. Slide your left hand down the inside of your left leg. Bend forward and place your left hand in front of your left foot and twist your torso to look up at your right hand as it stretches toward the ceiling. (If it is difficult to place the hand on the floor, you may place your hand to rest higher up on your left leg or use a stack of books). Inhale and look up toward your right hand as it stretches up toward the ceiling. Hold the pose for three deep breaths.

With each inhalation, feel your entire body expand with breath. With each exhalation, rotate your right pelvis so you feel the outside of your right foot on the floor. Continue to rest here for three deep inhalations and exhalations, concentrating on your breath.

When you are ready, inhale and slowly expand back up to center. Release your arms and legs for a moment and then repeat this pose to the other side.

Benefits of the *Triangle*:

The *Triangle* pose expands the chest and hip joints and strengthens the legs. It also expands the spinal column and is both energizing and centering for body and mind.

Twisting Triangle

Start with the same instructions for the Triangle pose on page 28. (Photos for the start-up poses are shown for the *Easy Triangle* on page 17).

Exhale as you twist toward your right side, bringing your left hand down to rest on the floor near the inside of your right foot. If this is difficult, you may place your hand higher up on the inside of your right leg or put a stack of books on the floor on the inside of your right foot and rest your hand on the stack of books. Exhale and stretch your right arm up. If it is comfortable, rest here for three breaths.

With each inhalation, elongate your spine and feel your entire body expand in all directions. With each exhalation, turn your hips a bit more to the right as you stretch your right arm up. When you have completed three deep breaths, inhale and expand back up to center.

Repeat this twist to the left side and hold it for three breaths. Then, inhale and expand back to center. Close your eyes and rest here for a few moments, enjoying the energizing effects of this deep twist.

Benefits of the *Twisting Triangle:*

The twisting triangle is a wonderful pose for strengthening the legs, opening the hips, and energizing the spine. The twisting movement tones the internal organs and restores energy to the upper body.

"Patience achieves everything."

Saint Teresa of Avila

Practicing Patience and Perseverance

Patience is a fast disappearing virtue in modern life. Children observe their parents and teachers rushing from one activity to another and assume that this is what they should do. Learning to slow down body and mind can help students develop the patience and perseverance needed to succeed in school.

Practicing patience requires simply being in the present moment. The experience of being rather than doing is often one of the most difficult things to find in the midst of a busy schedule.

Side Stretch at Desk

Sit tall in your chair with your feet flat on the floor. Inhale slowly as you raise your left arm and place your left hand on the top of your head. Exhaling, slowly bend to the left side.

Inhale as you return to center. This time as you inhale, observe the breath expanding all the way down the spine and feel yourself growing taller. Hold the

breath for a moment and concentrate on the base of your spine. Exhale slowly as you bend to the left side. Inhale as you slowly return to center. Repeat the same movement to the left side three times, coordinating each movement with the breath. When you have completed three deep breaths, inhale and return to center.

Now, repeat this movement to your right side. Remember to coordinate each movement with the breath. With each deep inhalation, feel the breath expanding the spine and the crown of your head lifting. With each slow exhalation, gently pull your head toward the side as you continue to expand up through the spine. Feel your neck expanding and the muscles along your spinal column relaxing. When you have completed three deep breaths, release your hand and gently massage your neck and shoulders.

Benefits of the *Side Stretch at desk:*

This simple stretch relieves tension in the neck and shoulders and quiets the mind. It is a simple pose that can easily be practiced anytime to help students slow down body and mind and practice patience.

Half Moon

Stand with your feet in a wide stance, about the length of one leg. Turn the left foot out 90 degrees and turn the right foot in slightly. Inhaling, press your thigh

muscles against the bones and straighten your kneecaps up to create a strong, sturdy base. Exhaling, draw your tailbone down and lengthen your spine up all the way to the top of the head. Inhaling, extend the arms to the sides with your palms toward the floor.

Exhale slowly and stretch to the left as far as possible. Place your left hand on a stack of books on the floor about twelve inches in front of your left foot and lift your right leg.

Inhale deeply as you extend your right hand up, expand your chest and lengthen your torso. Exhaling, extend through your arms and legs, down through your tailbone and up through your spine. Focus on a spot directly in front to help keep balance, lengthen the left leg, and bring the right leg up parallel to the floor. Notice that when your mind is still and focused you have more balance and control. (This is a more advanced balancing pose. If students find it difficult to balance, they may practice this pose with their back against a wall for support.)

Rest here for three deep breaths. With each inhalation, lengthen your arms, legs and spinal column to expand out in all directions from the center like a star. With each exhalation, raise your arm a bit higher as you open your chest. Again, breathe in deeply, feeling an expansion in your chest and shoulders. Exhaling, stretch the left arm down and place your fingertips about twelve inches in front of your left foot. Inhaling, lengthen your right arm up and fill your body with breath. Exhaling, stretch out through both legs, both arms, down through your tailbone and out through the top of your head. Rest here, breathing up and down your spine.

On the next exhalation, bend your left knee and place your right foot on the ground. Inhaling, expand back up into a wide stance standing position and repeat this pose with your right leg.

Benefits of the *Half Moon* pose:

The *Half Moon* pose frees the back and spine and helps release tension in the lower back and shoulders. It also enhances coordination, leg strength and flexibility in the hips and develops balance, concentration, patience and perseverance.

Double Silent Tree

Stand back-to-back with your partner and raise one foot, placing the sole of your foot against the inside of your opposite leg. Inhaling, raise your arms up to the side and hold hands with your partner.

Exhaling, press the palms of your hands together and stretch up through your spine. Inhaling, breathe into the hip joint of your bent leg. As you exhale slowly, let your bent knee move back more toward your partner's bent knee. On the next inhalation, raise your arms up to rest overhead together. Exhale slowly as you balance here with your partner.

Inhaling, breathe all the way down through the body. Imagine that your legs are the trunk of the tree, your arms the branches and your fingers the smaller twigs. Imagine that all the hairs on your head are the leaves of the tree. Listen to your leaves that are shimmering in the wind. Let your tree sway gently in the wind.

Now, feel the breath expand down through your trunk and into your feet. Imagine that you have roots that go deep into the earth. As you exhale, press down with your foot and feel your spine growing longer as if you are a tree that is growing.

Rest here for three deep breaths with your silent tree partner. When you are ready, gently lower your arms and bring your foot down. Then, repeat the tree pose with the other leg. Rest here for three breaths.

When you are ready, slowly lower your arms and bring your foot down. Rest here a few moments.

Benefits of the *Double Silent Tree*:

The tree pose develops concentration, balance and poise. It also strengthens the muscles in the legs, opens the hip joints and teaches patience.

Warrior

Stand with your feet in a wide stance. Your feet should be as far apart as the length of one of your own legs. Turn your right foot toward the right 90 degrees and your left foot to the right about 30 degrees. Keep the heel of your right foot in line with the arch of your left foot. Inhaling, raise your arms to shoulder level with the palms facing the floor. Turn your head to the right and feel your body lengthen from the middle of your back out through your fingertips.

Exhaling, bend your right knee until your thigh is parallel to the floor and your right knee is directly over your right ankle. To protect your knee, do not bring it in front of the right ankle. Make sure the knee stays in the center and does not collapse inward since this could put strain on the knee.

Stretch out through both hands, keeping the crown of your head in line with your tailbone. Hold the pose for three deep breaths, keeping your shoulders, neck and throat soft and relaxed as you breathe down into your legs and feet.

With each inhalation, feel strength and courage rising up through your strong legs and expanding through every part of your body. With each exhalation, let your body soften and allow the breath to become slower and softer. Continue to concentrate on the breath, with your body still as a mountain and the breath flowing like a river. When you have completed three breaths, inhale deeply as you expand back up to center. Exhale slowly as you release your arms.

Now, repeat the warrior pose to the other side. As you rest here for three deep breaths, concentrate completely on the breath. Feel it activating every muscle in your legs and bringing energy up into your heart to inspire courage and strength. Bring this courage and strength up through your legs and out through your arms.

When you have completed three deep breaths, inhale deeply as you return to center. Exhaling, slowly release your arms. Bring your feet to a parallel position, close your eyes and rest here a moment experiencing the effects of this pose.

Benefits of the *Warrior* pose:

The *Warrior* pose enhances endurance and strengthens the legs and back. It also tones the abdominal organs and brings energy up to the heart, inspiring courage and strength of spirit. This pose also focuses the mind and creates a strong, centered inner state.

Double Warrior

Stand side by side with your partner, facing opposite directions. Place your left foot next to his left foot. Place your right foot to the side about the distance of one of your own legs. Turn your right foot to the side 90 degrees with the heel of

your right foot in line with the arch of your left foot.

Inhaling, lift up through strong legs as you open your arms to the sides and grip your partner's arm. Lift your torso, neck and head and look over to your outside hand. Exhaling, bend your front leg and release the grip on your partner's arm, so your partner's hand slides down your arm to hold your wrist.

Rest here for three deep breaths. With each inhalation, continue to expand up through the top of your head and feel the breath expanding through the back leg and hip. Keep the front knee directly over the ankle. With each exhalation, pull away from your partner using the polarity created by this pull to stretch more through your front arm.

Rest here with your breath flowing like a river. With each deep inhalation, extend your arms to the side. Experience how this makes it easier to elongate your spine. With each long exhalation, pull gently against your partner, keeping the top of your head in line with the base of your spine.

When you are ready to come out of the pose, inhale as you straighten your front leg and return to center. Exhaling, walk your feet together, release your arms and repeat this pose to the other side.

Benefits of the *Double Warrior:*

This is a partner version of the traditional Yoga *Warrior* pose. Practicing this pose with a partner enhances the stretch because as you pull against your partner you use the polarity this creates to release deeper into the pose. It opens the shoulders, strengthens the legs, and develops balance and concentration. It also strengthens the lower body and raises energy into the heart. Just as a warrior must be trained so he will be successful on the battlefield, we will stay calm and centered amidst the pressures of daily life when we practice the art of keeping our inner poise.

Open the Window to Insight, Intuition and Inner Wisdom

"I shut my eyes in order to see."

Paul Gauguin

Given the high-tech world surrounding our children, sometimes a very simple movement or breathing exercise allows them to relax and learn how to access their innate inner qualities. The following exercises and breathing techniques are designed to inspire students to tap into their hidden treasures of insight, intuition and inner wisdom.

Intense Forward Stretch

Stand with your feet in a wide stance. Turn your right foot to the right 90 degrees and your left foot to the right 30 degrees. Inhaling, bring your arms behind your back and press the palms of your hands together.

Exhale slowly and turn your hips toward the right. Inhale. Again exhaling slowly, bend forward bringing your head toward your right knee.

Concentrate on the space between your eyebrows as you rest here for three deep breaths. With each inhalation, imagine that the breath comes in the space between your eyebrows. With each exhalation, let the breath become slower and softer.

After the third exhalation, inhale deeply as you roll up and release your arms. Now, repeat this pose to the other side.

Variation of the
Intense Forward Stretch

If it is difficult for you to bring your palms together behind your back, you may bring your arms behind your back and hold your forearms or elbows. Exhale slowly as you bend forward bringing your head toward your knee. Rest here for three deep breaths. Then, repeat this pose to the other side.

After the third exhalation, inhale deeply as you expand back up and release your arms. Rest here a few moments feeling the effects of this intense forward stretch.

Benefits of the
Intense Forward Stretch:

This intense forward stretch elongates the spine and allows it to relax. It enhances circulation in the upper body, nourishes the brain and calms the mind. Concentrating on the space between the eyebrows develops qualities of insight and intuition.

The Space between Each Breath

Sit in a comfortable position and close your eyes. Inhaling, observe your breath filling your entire body. Exhaling, allow the breath to become slower, softer and more subtle. Continue like this for a few breaths. Inhaling, breathe in deeply. Exhaling, breathe out long.

Now, begin to concentrate on the space between each breath. Inhale and concentrate on the space before the exhalation. Exhale and concentrate on the space before the inhalation. Continue like this on your own, sinking deeper and deeper into the subtle space between each breath. With each exhalation let your breath be slower and softer.

Benefits of the *Space between Each Breath* breathing:

This simple breathing exercise develops concentration and intuition. It also gives a rest to the mind, conserving its power. This is an easy and effective exercise to practice anytime the pressures of daily life create tension in the body and mind, obscuring vitality, stamina and joy.

Upside Down

Lie on your back with your lower legs resting on the seat of a chair. Breathe in deeply and raise your arms above your head to rest on the floor. As you exhale, slowly soften your shoulders and let them relax. Rest here for three deep breaths.

With each inhalation, feel the breath expand your rib cage and chest. Let each exhalation be slower and softer and feel your body relax more as you breathe out slowly.

Continue to rest in this pose as long as you like. With each exhalation, allow the breath to become slower and softer. Take a few more moments to enjoy this pose.

When you are ready to release this pose, bend your knees toward your chest, roll to your side and slowly sit up.

Benefits of *Upside Down*:

This restorative pose calms and revitalizes all the systems in the body. It releases tension in the back and soothes the nervous system. It is an easy way to dissolve fatigue and tension and harmonize body, mind, and emotions. The inverted position reverses the blood and lymph flow, gives a rest to the heart, and brings a great renewal of energy.

The ancient Yoga texts describe "Rasa" as the "nectar" or "bliss" that is inherent in all the Yoga poses. As you rest in this pose, it is easy to experience the subtle and relaxing effect of the "Rasa" or the feeling of well-being.

Young children generally adore this pose and students of all ages may also enjoy the rejuvenating effects of this pose for a few minutes during the school day to allow their bodies to rest while their minds absorb the information learned.

The Space between the Eyebrows Breathing Technique

Sit at your desk or with your forehead resting on a desk or on a book.

Close your eyes and imagine a window in the space between your eyebrows. Open the window and breathe in deeply. Exhaling, breathe out long. Visualize a stream of breath coming out the window in the space between your eyebrows. With each exhalation, let your breath be slower and softer. Rest here for several deep breaths and imagine a new way of seeing, with your eyes closed.

Benefits of the *Space between the Eyebrows* breathing exercise:

In the ancient texts on Hatha Yoga, the space between the eyebrows is called the "third eye." Concentrating on this space develops intuition.

FOUR

Concentration/Balance

"Yoga is the ability to direct the mind exclusively toward an object and to sustain this direction with no distraction."

Yoga Sutra 1.2

Enhancing Concentration

The movement and breathing exercises in this chapter are designed to develop skills of balance and concentration. By concentrating on the breath with each physical movement, students may develop the ability to be fully present in each moment and be able to concentrate for longer periods.

Nataraja

Stand with your feet parallel. Inhaling, extend your right arm to the front with your palm facing the floor. Exhaling, bend your left knee and grasp your left foot with

your left hand. If it is difficult to reach your foot with your hand, wrap a belt around your foot. To help keep your balance, look straight ahead, focusing your eyes on a specific point in front of you. Rest here for three deep breaths.

Inhaling, roll your shoulders back and down and expand your chest with breath. Exhaling, stretch your left arm and leg back and hold your left foot with your left hand. Rest in this position and breathe in deeply. As you breathe out long, roll your pelvis down until your hips are level. Inhale and breathe down your spine as you draw your tailbone down. Hold the breath in for a moment and concentrate on your coccyx. Exhale slowly as you lower your left leg. Now, repeat this pose with your other leg.

Benefits of *Nataraja*:

The *Nataraja* pose gives a wonderful psychological lift and enhances inner confidence and concentration. This balancing backbend also opens the chest and shoulders, strengthens the legs and cultivates balance and poise.

"The best things are very close: The air we breathe, the light in our eyes, the flowers at our feet, the tasks at hand."

Robert Louis Stevenson

The Tree

Stand with your feet in a parallel position. Inhale and raise your arms overhead as you lift your left foot, placing it on the inside of your right knee. Press your palms together above your head. As you rest here, imagine that you are a beautiful tree. As you breathe in, imagine the breath expanding all the way down through your legs and into your feet. Now imagine your have roots that go deep down into the earth. As you breathe out long, feel your tree growing taller. Continue to rest here concentrating on your breath for a few more deep breaths.

If you find it difficult to balance, you may practice the tree pose with your back against a wall.

When you are ready to come out of the pose, exhale slowly as you lower your leg and let your arms be light as leaves as they release down. Then, repeat the tree pose with your other leg.

Benefits of the *Tree*:

The *Tree* pose stretches the entire body, strengthens the legs and helps develop balance and concentration. The ancient Yoga texts explain our kinship with trees. Most children enjoy the tree pose and find it fun to imagine that they are different kinds of trees, with their leaves shimmering in the wind and their roots going deep into the earth.

The Eagle

Stand with your feet parallel. Inhale and stretch your arms out to the sides at shoulder level. Exhaling, lengthen your arms out through your fingertips and feel the opening in your back and shoulders. Inhaling, bend your knees slightly and lift your right leg, crossing it as high as possible over your left leg, and wrap your right foot around your left calf. Exhaling, lengthen your upper body.

Inhaling, cross your right arm over your left arm above the elbows. Exhaling, wrap your right arm around your left so the back of your palms touch. Now, if it is easy for you, wrap one hand around the other to bring your palms together. If this is difficult, keep your hands in the first position with the backs of your hands together.

On the next inhalation, lengthen your spine and concentrate on the coccyx. Exhaling, visualize the breath expanding into your arms, legs and entire body and imagine you are becoming strong as an eagle. Rest here for three deep breaths, concentrating on the strength and freedom of an eagle. On the third exhalation, slowly release your arms and bring the right down to stand with the feet in a parallel position.

Now, repeat the *Eagle* pose with your other leg and rest here for three deep breaths. On the third exhalation, slowly release your arms and bring your left leg down to stand with the feet in a parallel position. Close your eyes and rest here a few moments, observing the breath and the effects of the pose.

Benefits of the *Eagle*:

The *Eagle* pose gives a deep stretch to the shoulders and upper back. Practice this pose after sitting at a desk or writing for some time since it opens the chest and stretches the arms and hands. It also stretches the legs, increases flexibility in the joints and enhances concentration.

Double Boat

Sit facing your partner with your legs open wide and place the soles of your feet together. Hold your partner's hands. Now, gently press your feet against your partner's and slowly raise your legs together at the same time.

Stretch up through your spine as you continue to press your feet and pull gently against your partner's hands to keep your balance. Bravo!

Benefits of the *Double Boat:*

The *Boat* pose expands the spine, and strengthens the muscles in the legs and lower abdomen. It also develops balance, poise, and concentration.

Golden Channel Breathing Technique

Lie on your back with your legs and feet resting on a Yoga ball or rest your legs on the seat of a chair. This exercise may also be done sitting in a chair.

Close your eyes and observe your breath. As you inhale, visualize your breath expanding down your spine. Hold your breath in for a moment and concentrate on your coccyx. Exhale slowly and concentrate on your breath as it rises back up through each vertebra of your spine. Rest here for three deep breaths.

On the next inhalation, imagine a channel of golden light descending through each vertebra of your spine. Hold your breath in for a moment and concentrate on the base of your spine. Exhaling, visualize

your breath rising back up through each vertebra. Continue to concentrate on your breath as it expands up and down the golden channel of your spine. With each exhalation, let your breath become slower and more subtle. Experience that, as your breath becomes more subtle, your body feels lighter.

Continue to enjoy this subtle and energizing breath for as long as you like, then rest here a few moments with your eyes closed to enjoy the soothing effect of this pose.

Benefits of the *Golden Channel Breathing Technique:*

This restorative inverted pose gives a rest to the legs, increases circulation in the upper body, and refreshes both body and mind. The reversed blood flow gives a rest to the heart and soothes the nervous system. This is an effective exercise for teaching students one pointed focus and enhancing their ability to concentrate for longer periods. Practicing this pose with a partner creates a feeling of harmony and union.

Experiencing the present moment

"Today is the tomorrow you worried about yesterday."
  Anonymous

One of the easiest ways to experience the present moment is to concentrate on the breath while practicing simple movements in coordination with the breath. As the breath slows down, the mind becomes calm and it is easier to become so aware of the present in each position that everything else fades away. When students experience this total absorption, they effortlessly enter the present moment.

Arm Stretch at Desk

Inhale and raise your arms to the sides. As you exhale, let your arms become lighter and grow longer and stretch them over your head.

Rest here for three deep breaths. With each inhalation, imagine your arms growing longer from inside. Exhaling slowly, soften your shoulders and relax them back and down. Breathe in deeply, concentrating completely on the breath as your arms stretch up a bit higher. As you exhale slowly, gently squeeze the muscles deep in your abdomen and lift your arms a little higher. On the next inhalation, bring your arms up alongside your ears. Exhaling, release your shoulders back and down as your arms continue to grow longer.

After you have completed three deep breaths, inhale and visualize your breath expanding down through your legs and into your feet. Let the exhalation be very soft and slow and feel your arms becoming lighter as they slowly expand down.

Close your eyes for a moment. How do your arms and upper body feel?

Benefits of the *Arm Stretch*:

This stretch releases tension in the shoulders, neck, and arms. It also slows down body and mind and teaches how to concentrate on the breath.

Penguin Stretch

Stand with your feet parallel. Inhaling, raise your arms up over your head and bring your palms together. Stretch up through your hands and feel the breath expand your chest and rib cage as you lengthen up.

Exhaling, fall forward and bring your palms down between your legs and stretch them as far back as comfortable.

Dynamic version

Repeat this movement three times, coordinating each movement with the breath. Inhale deeply each time you return to the vertical position. Exhale long each time you bend forward into the deep forward stretch. Concentrate completely on the breath, allowing it to move your body in one continuous motion. When you have completed the movement three times, inhale slowly as you return to a standing position.

Static version

Exhale and fall forward, bringing your hands between your knees and as far back behind your body as comfortable. Rest here for three deep breaths. With each inhalation, feel your chest and rib cage expand with breath. With each exhalation, release your head and neck as you stretch your arms more toward the back.

When you have completed three deep breaths, inhale deeply and stretch up through your arms as you return to a standing position. Exhaling, slowly release your arms back down to rest at your sides.

Close your eyes and rest here for a few moments to experience the effects of this deep forward stretch.

Benefits of the *Penguin Stretch:*

This intense forward bend stretches the back of the legs and allows the spinal column to elongate and relax. It brings an increased supply of blood to the upper body, releases the shoulders and neck, nourishes the brain and enhances concentration, especially when practiced in coordination with the breath.

Hair-Raising Stretch

Stand with your feet in a wide stance, about the length of one leg. Inhaling, place your hands on your hips and stretch your spine. Exhaling, slowly bend forward, keeping your spine long. Place your hands on the outside of your legs or ankles and relax your head and shoulders.

Rest here, breathing deeply. With each inhalation, lengthen your spine and expand your chest with breath. With each exhalation, let your breath become slower, softer and more subtle and feel your head release more toward the floor. As you rest here breathing deeply, relax your face and close your eyes. Keep your legs strong as your torso releases more forward with each exhalation.

When you are ready to come up, inhale slowly as you return to center. Close your eyes and rest here for a few moments, observing the breath and the effects of the pose.

Benefits of the *Hair-Raising Stretch*:

The *Hair-Raising* stretch increases circulation to the head, which stimulates the brain, and the pituitary gland. It is beneficial for the health of the hair and the complexion, keeps the hip joints limber, stretches the hamstrings and strengthens the legs. This pose also tones the internal organs and is recommended for relieving stomach pains. The increased supply of blood to the upper body also revitalizes the thousands of nerve endings in the spinal column and calms the mind.

The Boat

Sit with your legs extended to the front. Inhale as you bend your knees and grasp the arches of your feet with your hands.

Exhale slowly as you raise your legs a few inches off the floor. Fix your gaze on a point in front of you to help keep your balance. As you hold this pose for three breaths, concentrate on the breath expanding up and down your spinal column. With each inhalation, feel your spine elongating. With each exhalation, lift your legs a little higher, until they are as high as possible without straining.

Now release your hands and extend your arms and legs.

Remember, always respect your own body and find the version of the pose that is comfortable for you.

When you have completed three breaths, exhale slowly as you release your legs.

Benefits of the *Boat Pose*:

The *Boat* pose develops balance and concentration. It also stretches the spine and strengthens the muscles in the legs and lower abdomen.

Be the Witness Breathing Technique

Rest your head on your desk or on books on your desk. Rest here a few moments and observe your breath.

Something deep inside you knows that you are alive, that you are breathing and thinking. It is your awareness. This "witness" is always there and is the basis of everything you experience. It watches and knows everything you do. Yet, it is so subtle that it is often taken for granted.

Sit quietly and watch your thoughts as if they are a movie. Tune into the part of you that is watching your thoughts, witnessing them.

Now, observe your breath. Inhale and breathe in deeply. Exhale and let your body and mind relax. Who is it that knows you are breathing?

When you fall asleep and dream and then wake up, who is it that remembers your dream?

Rest here quietly for a few minutes and be aware of that part of you that is always the witness. Experience that this "witness" is always there right inside you.

Benefits of *Be the Witness Breathing Technique:*

This simple and ancient breathing technique teaches students how to focus the mind and improve concentration. It also gives the mind a rest, creates a calm peaceful feeling and is soothing for the nervous system.

"All knowledge can be known in the vivid light of intuition."
Yoga Sutra 111.34

Balancing Activity with Quiet Time

The *Yoga Sutra* describes how the "hridayam" or heart center is considered to be the seat of the mind. This ancient Sanskrit text explains that, when we are able to access the wisdom of the heart center, an inherent intelligence that is beyond ordinary understanding based on words or cognitive processes, our mental capacity is greatly enhanced.

Experiencing this deeper wisdom is much easier when we are quiet and calm. As Patanjali, the author of the *Yoga Sutra* explains it, "One cannot see the color of a lake when it is agitated." Stillness and quiet are as essential as action and movement. Yet, it is not always easy for children to find quiet time and stillness. In their daily lives they are often bombarded with stimuli of all kinds and sometimes feel as stressed as their teachers and parents.

By taking time for a few slow movements and breathing exercises, teachers may encourage students to appreciate silence and stillness. This quiet time may be used to teach students techniques that they may use to relax their body and mind, enabling them to experience an inner stillness that gives them access to their intuition and innate wisdom. This understanding is beyond ordinary knowledge based on words or rational thought processes.

The Bridge

Lie on your back with your knees bent and your feet flat on the floor. Breathe in as you lift your hips and press your feet on the floor. Breathe out slowly as you lift your hips a little higher. Now, bring your hands togeth-

er at the base of your spine and rest here for a few breaths. Imagine that your body is as strong as a bridge and that your breath is flowing like a river.

When you are ready to release this pose, bring your arms to rest alongside your body and exhale as you slowly roll down.

Benefits of the *Bridge*:

This soothing pose massages the thousands of nerve endings in the spinal column and tones the abdominal organs. It helps to correct round shoulders and creates a strong flexible spine, preparing the body for the more advanced poses. It is calming and centering for both body and mind.

Lunge

Rest on all fours. Inhale as you step your left foot forward between your hands, stretch your arms up alongside your ears and look up.

Rest here for three deep breaths. With each inhalation, stretch up with your arms and feel the breath expand your rib cage and chest. With each exhalation, let your breath become slower, softer and more subtle.

When you have completed three deep breaths, exhale slowly as you release your arms, step your left foot back and return to rest on all fours.

Now repeat the lunge with your other leg. When you have completed three deep breaths, exhale slowly as you release your arms, step your right foot back and sit back to rest on your heels.

Benefits of the *Lunge*:

The *Lunge* opens the hip joints and strengthens the legs. It also releases tension in the neck and shoulders and opens the chest, encouraging deeper breathing. It is relaxing and soothing for both body and mind.

Waterfall

Stand with your feet about eighteen inches apart. Inhaling, stretch your arms up alongside your ears and arch back as you look toward the sky.

Exhaling, bend your knees and fall forward, bringing your fingertips to touch the floor.

Rest here for three deep breaths. With each inhalation, visualize your rib cage and lower back expanding with breath. With each exhalation, release your head and neck and feel your body relax more into the pose.

When you have completed the third exhalation, slowly inhale as you return to a standing position. Close your eyes and rest here a few moments to experience the effects of this pose.

Benefits of the *Waterfall*:

This deep forward bend stretches the muscles in the backs of the legs. It also allows the spinal column to lengthen and release. The active stretch of the legs allows for a passive release of the torso and brings an increased supply of blood to relax the upper body.

The Grape Press

Lie on your back with your hips facing your partner's hips. Inhaling, bend your knees up and bring the soles of your feet up to press against your partner's feet.

Rest here, breathing together as you gently press the soles of your feet against each other.

As you breathe in deeply, imagine that the breath is expanding all the way through your body down into your legs and into your feet. Hold the breath in for a moment and feel your feet gently pressing against your partner's feet. Exhale long and slowly as you continue to feel the soles of your feet pressing against one another. With each exhalation, let your breath become slower and softer.

Rest here for three deep breaths, enjoying a few moments of silent connection.

Benefits of the *Grape Press*:

This restful pose soothes the nervous system and calms both body and mind.

Open the Window Breathing Technique

Sit back on your heels and bring your forehead to the floor.

Close your eyes and imagine a window in the space between your eyebrows. Open the window and breathe in deeply. Exhaling,

breathe out slowly. Feel the subtle stream of breath come out the window in the space between the eyebrows. Rest here for several deep breaths and imagine a new way of seeing, with your eyes closed.

Benefits of *Open the Window Breathing Technique:*

This restful pose refreshes both body and mind. Concentrating on the space between the eyebrows, sometimes called the third eye, develops intuition. Practicing this pose together creates a feeling of harmony and union.

FIVE

Harmony/Friendship

"May we be united in our hearts. May we be united in our thoughts.
May there be perfect unity between us."

Rig Veda 10:194

This chapter presents individual, partner, and group poses that students may practice together. Group practice has a harmonizing effect. By synchronizing their movements and breathing, students may discover that the source of harmony and friendship is the silent connection that is always there.

The partner poses presented in this chapter are designed to enhance strength, concentration, and inspire deeper friendships. Through practicing partner poses, students may experience that it is possible to accomplish more by working together than by working on their own as they share a glimpse of the unity inherent in all creation.

Building Trust and Friendship

Children love interaction. This section presents a series of playful partner poses that encourage students to learn trust and cooperation as they explore ways of supporting each other. Practicing with a partner enables them to stretch more than possible while practicing on their own. Partner poses are emotionally nourishing, enhance relationships and teach children how to be sensitive to others and learn how to adjust to the needs of others.

"The most beautiful things in the world are not seen or heard, they are felt with the heart."

Helen Keller

Circle of Friendship

Sit in a circle with the sides of your feet touching your friends' lower legs.

Dynamic version

Inhale and raise your arms up alongside your ears. As you exhale slowly, bend forward, bringing all your hands on top of each other in the center of the circle. Inhale deeply, return to an upright seated position with

your arms stretched up alongside your ears. Exhale slowly as you lower your arms. Repeat this movement for three deep inhalations and exhalations.

Static version

Inhale and raise your arms up alongside your ears. As you exhale slowly, bend forward bringing all your hands on top of each other in the center of the circle. Rest here for three deep inhalations and three slow exhalations. With each inhalation, feel your torso expand with breath. With each exhalation, feel your body release more toward the center of the circle. When you have completed three deep breaths, return to an upright seated position with your arms stretched up alongside your ears. Exhale and slowly lower your arms.

Circle of Friendship Game

You may also use the circle of friendship to play a game. To begin, players inhale and raise their arms up alongside their ears. Then, one child calls out "exhale left," "exhale right" or "exhale center" and everyone follows this command. The same person then calls out "inhale back up," and everyone returns to the starting position. Then the next child takes a turn being the leader who calls out the direction.

Two Frogs on a Lotus

Sit in a squatting position opposite your partner. Reach your arms forward to hold hands with your partner. Keep your arms alongside your ears and breathe in deeply. Feel your spinal column expand.

Now, concentrate on the tailbone at the base of your spine and imagine you have a heavy tail. Breathe out long and feel your tail gently move a bit closer to the floor as your arms gently pull against your partner's arms. Close your eyes and concentrate on your breath for a few moments.

Benefits of *Two Frogs on a Lotus:*

This pose releases the hip joints, opens the shoulder joints and expands the spinal column, creating space between the vertebrae. It also teaches how to use polarity and counterbalance, giving students an experience of true teamwork.

The Toboggan

Partner One sits behind Partner Two, putting his feet on her lower back, giving a little massage to warm up the muscles in the lower back.

Now, Partner One places his left foot on her lower back and his right foot on the center of her back at heart level.

As she raises her arms and stretches them backward, gently hold her wrists. Exhaling, very gently pull her arms back. Inhaling, she breathes into her chest. As you exhale together, softly press your feet more into her back enhancing the stretch.

Rest here, breathing together. With each inhalation, let your spine expand. With each exhalation, pull gently, allowing her to relax more into the pose.

After three deep breaths, release her hands. As she bends forward, gently massage her lower back with your feet. Then turn around and reverse positions and repeat this pose.

Benefits of the *Toboggan*:

This pose expands the chest and opens the shoulder joints. It also releases tension in the neck and shoulders and develops the ability to be sensitive to the needs of each other and work together.

Twin Triangle

Stand back to back with your feet about four feet apart. Open your arms to the sides at shoulder level and stretch them to the sides.

Rest here a few moments, synchronizing your breath with your partner's. On the inhalation, breathe in deeply and feel your chest and rib cage expand. Exhaling, expand up through your spine and out through your arms.

On the next inhalation, turn your front foot out 90 degrees and your back foot in about 30 degrees. Exhaling, slide your hand down to rest on your partner's lower leg. Inhaling, press the palm of your top hand into your partner's palm and look up.

Rest here for three deep breaths. With each inhalation, continue to stretch up through your top hand and down through your bottom hand. At the same time, elongate your spine and stretch up through your head. With each exhalation, press you palms against your partner's palms and rotate your chest toward the sky.

When you have completed three deep breaths, expand back up on the next inhalation by lifting your top hand toward the sky. Exhaling slowly, release your arms and walk your feet together. Repeat this pose to your other side.

Benefits of the *Twin Triangle*:

The *Triangle* pose is a classic Yoga pose that strengthens the legs, opens the shoulders and creates a deep release in the hip joints. It also releases tension in the shoulders and neck, expands the spine and tones the spinal nerves. It stimulates the appetite and improves digestion. Practicing this pose with a partner makes it easier to keep the body in one plane and perform this pose with proper alignment.

Friendship Chair

Partner One, sit with your legs extended in front of you. Partner Two, lie down on your back with your hips touching your partner's lower back and the backs of your legs resting against his upper back and head.

Breathe in deeply and imagine the breath expanding through your body and into your legs and feet. As you exhale, let all your muscles soften and relax. Feel how this pose reverses the blood flow in your body, giving your heart a rest and making you feel very calm.

Benefits of the *Friendship Chair*:

This pose gives a rest to the heart and drains the lymph glands in the legs. The inverted position takes the weight off the legs and calms the mind. It is a good pose to enhance cooperation and friendship.

The Circle of Giving and Receiving

While practicing the partner poses in this section, students use the weight of their body to create support and counterbalance. This enables them to help each other stretch more into the poses than they could on their own, giving them a direct experience of true teamwork.

"Give and receive. If you wish to receive, give first."

Zen Proverb

Forward Backbend

Sit back to back with your partner with your legs extended in front of you. Stretch your arms to your sides and take hold of your partner's hands.

Partner One, hold your partner's hands and slowly bend forward, allowing your partner's torso and head to rest on your back. With each inhalation, let the breath expand your body and feel your back expand against your partner's back. With each exhalation, gently pull your partner forward a little more.

Rest here, breathing together for several breaths. With each inhalation, stretch your legs and feet. Open your chest and breathe into your lower back, feeling it expand against your partner's lower back. With every exhalation, let your body soften as your partner pulls you a bit further into the pose.

When you are ready, slowly return to center and reverse roles.

Benefits of the *Forward Backbend*:

This is a beginning backbend that gives support to the muscles of the back while training the spine to bend. It opens the chest and helps make the spine flexible, preparing it for the more advanced poses. This pose is emotionally nourishing and teaches trust and cooperation.

Sailboat Stretch

Sit facing your partner with your legs open wide. Put the bottoms of your feet together and hold your partner's left hand.

Now, open your sails by stretching your right arm toward the back. Gently, pull away from your partner and look back at your right hand.

Close your eyes and imagine you are sailing through a big blue ocean.

Benefits of the *Sailboat Stretch*:

The *Sailboat Stretch* opens the shoulder joints, stretches the muscles in the arms and expands the spine. The twisting motion massages all the internal organs. It gives a powerful experience of the principles of polarity and gives students the experience that it is easier to stretch more when practicing with a partner.

Twin Spinal Twist

Sit facing your partner with your legs crossed and your knees touching your partner's knees. Inhale and stretch your left arm forward and wrap your right hand around your back. With your left hand reach to the right to take your partner's left hand. Exhale slowly as you twist to the right and look over your right shoulder. Rest here for three breaths.

As you breathe in deeply, feel your entire torso expand with breath. Exhaling, gently pull your partner's hand as you twist more toward the right. Again, inhale deeply feeling the breath expand your spinal column. Exhaling, gently press your knees against your partner's knees as you twist more to the right from the base of your spine. On the third inhalation, feel how the space inside your body is light and expanded. On the last exhalation, feel how your body is so soft and relaxed that it naturally releases further into the twist with the exhalation.

On the next inhalation, return to center and repeat this twist to the other side. As you rest in the pose for three long deep breaths, remember to let your body expand with each inhalation. Let each exhalation be softer, slower and more subtle and feel your body effortlessly release deeper into the twist with each breath.

After the third long slow exhalation, inhale deeply as you return to center. Close your eyes and rest here a few minutes to experience the effects of this twist.

Benefits of the *Twin Spinal Twist*:

This pose helps release tension in the lower back, opens the shoulders and increases spinal flexibility. It also stimulates spinal nerves and ligaments, enhances digestion and massages all the abdominal organs. It provides a kinesthetic experience of the natural circle of giving and receiving.

Standing Back-to-Back Twist

Stand back-to-back with your partner. Inhaling, raise your arms to the sides and take hold of your partner's hands.

As you exhale slowly, twist to one side, synchronizing your breath and your movement with your partner's breath and movement.

Inhale slowly as you and your partner return to center together. Exhaling again, twist to the opposite side. Continue like this for several breaths, moving from side to side in one continuous motion with the breath.

Benefits of the *Standing Back-to-Back Twist*:

This simple twist teaches students how to synchronize the breath with the twist and brings a renewal of energy. It also expands the spine, stretches the muscles of the arms and tones the internal organs. It teaches students to tune into their partner and be sensitive to the needs of each other.

The Moving Pillow Breathing Technique

Lie on your back and place the back of your head on your friends' abdomen as you open your arms to the side.

Inhale deeply and feel your abdomen expand with breath as if you are blowing up a balloon. Exhale slowly and feel your abdomen deflate completely. Rest here, concentrating on your breath. With each inhalation, expand your abdomen with breath and feel your friend's abdomen expand against the back of your head. With each exhalation, let your breath become slower and more subtle. Continue to breathe deeply and concentrate completely on your breath as you rest here. Feel each inhalation expanding all the way down into your abdomen. With each exhalation, observe your abdomen deflate.

Continue at your own rhythm for a few more deep breaths. As you practice this deep breathing, observe your breath becoming slower and softer.

Benefits of the *Moving Pillow:*

Deep breathing brings a fresh supply of oxygen to the lungs, blood, heart and brain. It also has a beneficial and soothing effect on the nervous system. Practicing this pose together creates a feeling of harmony and connection.

Creating a Harmonious Classroom

This section presents several poses that everyone in the class may practice together. By doing simple movements together, coordinated with the breath, you and your class may enjoy an enhanced experience of harmony and friendship, and experience the union that is the essence of Yoga.

Stretch Up

Sit in a chair with your feet flat on the floor. Inhaling, stretch your arms up and interlock your fingers above your head with your palms turned up.

Exhaling, rest here and feel your arms growing longer. On the next inhalation, lengthen up through your spine.

Exhale slowly and bend to your right side. Inhaling, stretch your arms up a bit higher as you return to center.

Exhale slowly as you stretch toward your left side. Inhale deeply as you return to center. Continue to stretch from side to center to the other side for three deep breaths. With each inhalation, feel the extension through the arms as they stretch up higher and higher. With each exhalation, let your body release more toward the side.

When you have completed three deep breaths, exhale as you slowly lower your arms. Feel your arms becoming lighter and lighter as they slowly come down.

Benefits of the *Stretch Up:*

This simple pose can be practiced anytime to release tension in the back and shoulders. It expands the rib cage and teaches students how to breathe deeply. The entire class may practice it together, and by synchronizing their breath and movements, experience harmony and unity of group.

Seated Forward Bend

Sit in your chair with your feet flat on the floor. Exhale and slowly bend forward, bringing your chest down to rest on your thighs and your hands down to rest on top of your feet. Close your eyes and rest here for three deep breaths.

With each inhalation, feel your body growing bigger from inside. With each exhalation, let your head release more toward your feet and feel your entire body soften as all the tension in your shoulders and neck dissolves.

When you are ready to release the pose, inhale deeply as you return to an upright position. Keep your eyes closed and sit her for a few moments to experience the effects of this restful pose.

Benefits of the *Seated Forward Bend*:

This relaxing pose releases tension in the neck and shoulders, stretches the lower back and calms the mind.

Cobbler's Stretch

Sit facing your partner in the *Cobbler's* pose. Partner One, sit with the soles of your feet together. Partner Two, bring the soles of your feet to rest on the top of your partner's feet. Stretch your arms forward to take hold of each other's wrists.

Inhaling, Partner One, gently lean back, pulling your partner toward you. Exhaling, Partner Two, lean back, pulling your partner toward you. As you continue to move back and forth in a continuous motion with the breath, elongate your spine. Continue like this for several breaths.

Benefits of the *Cobbler's Stretch*:

The *Cobbler's* pose is a traditional Yoga pose that releases the hip joints. The rocking motion enhances the extension in the spine, opens the shoulders, stretches the inner thigh muscles and encourages breathing into the back of the body.

Back to Back Breathing Technique

Sit back to back with your partner and cross your legs. Place the palms of your hands to rest on your thighs, just above your knees. Scoot together so your tailbones are touching and your spines are in line with each other. Close your eyes and breathe in deeply. Feel the breath go all the way down into the small of your back and feel the small of your back expand with breath until it touches your partner's back.

Take a few minutes to concentrate on your breath and synchronize your breath with your partner's breath. Exhale together, breathing through the nostrils. Inhaling, breathe in deeply, filling your body with breath and energy. Again, exhale slowly with your partner. On the next inhalation, feel the breath expand your back against your partner's back. Continue to synchronize your breath with your partner's breath, enjoying a few minutes of silent connection.

Benefits of *Back to Back Breathing:*

This simple breathing exercise expands breathing capacity and enhances the experience of unity and partnership.

Pink Cloud Contemplation

Sit with your eyes closed and imagine a beautiful pink cloud. Put your thoughts or worries on the pink cloud and visualize the cloud floating away.

S I X

Joy/Contentment

"There is only one duty, and that is to be happy."
Diderot

Children have a great capacity for joy. Their ability to play makes fun and joy a natural part of Yoga. When they laugh and have fun, their bodies and minds spontaneously relax. Teachers can cultivate this innate ability. This chapter presents a series of exercises designed to allow children to express their joy, present their own variations, or create their own unique poses.

Let's "Play" Yoga

It is essential to present Yoga to children in a way that is attractive and fun. Encourage your students to develop their imagination and "play" Yoga. There are many possibilities for using Yoga exercises to develop the imagination and inspire children to express their joy.

The following list will give you an idea of some ways you and your students may "play" Yoga.

Creative Ideas for "Playing" Yoga

- Each child makes a drawing of a Yoga pose. This may be a simple stick drawing, a real body drawing or a creative drawing.

- Each child holds up his or her drawing and the other students try to name the pose.

- Each child "teaches" the pose in his or her drawing to the class.

- The students create a "Yoga" choreography to music. As each child does his or her own pose, the other students follow as the pose of each student evolves into another students pose in one continuous flow or "Vinyasa."

- Each child chooses a drawing from another classmate and then leads the class in this pose.

- The students break up into small groups and make up a story that is told with their bodies. The sequence of individual poses tells their story.

- All the drawings are kept on a board in the classroom. Each morning, a different student chooses the poses that the class will do during their Yoga breaks that day.

- One or more of the daily Yoga breaks may be a time for improvisation when students create their own poses or partner poses and then share them with each other. Children love to create their own poses and this exercise develops creativity and self-confidence.

You and your class may use your own imagination and creativity to create your own Yoga fun!

Bursting with Joy

For children, Yoga is another form of play. It is essential to present Yoga to young children in a way that is fun and playful. They do not need to have perfect alignment or perfect positions. Children love to create their own poses and often spontaneously do their own unique version of a pose.

"We do not always need to go to a mountain to learn fromthe sages. Everything I needed to know, I learned from children..."

Romano Guardini

Bursting into Blossom

Sit with the soles of your feet together. Inhale as you slide your hands under your legs and lift up your legs like a flower that is growing. As you exhale slowly, open your hands like a flower that is bursting into blossom.

Rest here for three deep breaths. With each inhalation, feel your flower grow taller. With each exhalation, feel your flower becoming happier.

Benefits of *Bursting into Blossom*:

This pose expands the spinal column and stretches the legs. It also teaches balance and concentration.

Growing Sunflower

Start in a squatting position and rest on your toes. Inhale deeply and bring your elbows and forearms together in front of your chest. Exhaling, open your hands so your palms face up.

As you rest here for three deep breaths, imagine you are a flower that is growing taller in the summer sun. With each inhalation, feel your spinal column expand. With each exhalation, imagine joy and contentment growing inside you.

Benefits of the *Growing Sunflower:*

This pose expands the spine, opens the hip joints and strengthens all the muscles in the legs. It also enhances balance and concentration.

Double Dancers

Stand on the floor facing your partner. Lift your inside arm up and hold hands with your partner. This will help you keep your balance as you lift your opposite leg, bend the knee and hold your ankle with your hand.

As you balance here, let your breath flow downward and imagine that you have roots that go deep into the earth. Rest here for several deep breaths, then slowly release your arm and leg, reverse positions and try it with your other leg.

Benefits of the *Double Dancer:*

This pose develops balance and concentration and makes the back and legs more flexible.

Tango Twist

Stand back-to-back with your feet about four feet apart. Inhaling, stretch your arms to the sides at shoulder level. Exhale and clasp your hands together.

Turn your front foot toward the front 90 degrees and your back foot in about 30 degrees. Inhaling, stretch your front hands behind your back toward your back leg as you rotate your torso until your inside shoulder is next to your partner's inside shoulder.

Exhaling, raise your back arms up and stretch them to the front. Rest here, breathing together.

Adjust your feet so the hips are touching and extend your front arms toward the front and your back arms toward the back. Enjoy the nice stretch all the way down the inside of your arms. On the inhalation, pull your tailbone down to elongate your spine.

As you extend upward through the top of your head and downward through the base of your spine, stretch out from side to side with your arms. Feel the wonderful polarity this creates, freeing your neck and allowing your body to release further into the pose. Rest here with your body still as a mountain and your breath flowing like a dancer's.

When you are ready to come out of the pose, release your front arms and lift your back arms upward. Exhaling, release your front arm and swing back around to stand back to back with your partner. Rest here a few moments, observing the breath and the warmth in your shoulder joints. Then, repeat the tango twist to the other side.

Benefits of the *Tango Twist*:

This pose tones the muscles of the arms, opens the shoulder joints, and strengthens the legs and lower body. It creates a lightness of spirit and melts winter blues.

Creativity Flows From a Quiet Mind

"Real education is that which enables one to utilize the knowledge acquired for making happy as many people as possible."

Sai Baba

Giving students a few moments of quiet time each day may give them a precious opportunity to learn to navigate their own inner highway and allow them to discover the source of creativity. The exercises in this section are designed to encourage teachers to give their students time to practice tuning into this unique aspect and encourage its full expression.

Sun-Moon Breath

Lie with your legs on the ball or on a chair.

Close your eyes and follow your breath up and down your spine. With each inhalation, visualize your breath coming in the center top of your head and moving all the way down your spine. Hold it in for a moment and concentrate on your coccyx.

Exhaling, follow the breath as it flows back up your spine. Let your breath go at its own rhythm. Simply observe it as it moves up and down the channel of your spine.

Benefits of the *Sun-Moon Breath*:

The ancient texts of Hatha Yoga describe how there are two major subtle nerve channels in the spine. Breathing up and down the spine unites these two channels, enhancing our experience of well-being and unity.

These ancient texts equated the heating or dynamic energy of the body with the sun and the cooling or restorative energy with the moon. They explain that one purpose of Hatha Yoga is to unite these two energies through certain postures. Regular practice of the Sun-Moon Breath balances these two energies and teaches students how to tap into the source of creativity.

Cloudless Sky Contemplation

Close your eyes and imagine you are looking at a cloudless sky. Rest here, enjoying that stillness.

Cultivating Contentment

The ancient texts on Yoga explain how contentment is a quality that must be cultivated. In the same way that we must make an effort to maintain our physical body and keep it healthy, it is essential to take time to nourish psychological needs.

"The result of contentment is total happiness."

Yoga Sutra 11.42

The movement and breathing exercises presented in this section are designed to teach students how to develop a state of inner contentment that will sustain them through the daily demands of competitive education, allowing them to succeed at school, and to maintain a positive attitude.

Butterfly

Sit with the soles of your feet together and your knees open to the sides. Inhale as you place your hands on your shoulders and lift your elbows. Exhaling, lower your arms and press your knees toward the floor.

Continue to flap your butterfly wings like this for several deep breaths. With each inhalation, expand your chest and lift your wings. With each exhalation, lower your wings and press your knees toward the floor. Imagine you are a beautiful butterfly flying through the flowers.

When you are ready to rest, exhale and slowly release your arms. Close your eyes and rest here for a few moments.

Benefits of the *Butterfly*:

This joyful pose opens the hip and shoulder joints and relaxes all the muscles in the shoulders and back of the neck. It soothes the nervous system and creates a feeling of calm contentment.

The Laughing Table

Sit on the floor and place the palms of your hands on the floor behind your body. Place the soles of your feet flat on the floor in front of you. As you exhale, push on your hands and feet and lift your torso until your body looks like a table. Make sure that your hands are directly under your shoulders and your feet are under your knees. As you rest here for three deep breaths, imagine that you are a laughing table.

When you are ready to release this pose, breathe out slowly as you sit back down on the floor.

Benefits of the *Table* pose:

The table pose strengthens the arms, opens the chest and corrects round shoulders. It also develops confidence and inspires students to discover an inner strength.

Soothing Stretch

Stand with your feet parallel. Inhaling, expand your arms up to the sides and over your head.

Exhaling, flex your palms and bend forward, imagining that your flexed palms are sliding down a window pane.

If it is comfortable for you, rest in the forward bend with your palms flat on the floor for three deep breaths. With each inhalation, feel your entire body expand with breath and contentment. With each exhalation, let your breath become softer and more subtle and observe your body effortlessly releasing more forward.

When you are ready to release this pose, inhale as you return to a standing position with your arms above your head. Exhaling, feel your arms become lighter and lighter as they slowly release down to rest at your sides. Close your eyes and rest here a few moments.

Benefits of the *Soothing Stretch*:

This deep forward bend brings an increased supply of blood to the upper body and nourishes the brain. It also stretches the arms and wrist joints, soothes the nervous system and creates a feeling of calm contentment.

Cultivating Contentment Breathing Technique

Lie down in front of a wall, bend your knees and roll to one side. Keep your knees bent into your chest as you turn onto your back. Scoot your hips forward until they touch the wall and extend your legs upward to rest against the wall.

As you rest here for three deep breaths, imagine cool blue water cascading down your legs to make a crystal blue pool in your abdomen, then visualize that this blue liquid drains down into your head and feel it streaming out through the arms.

Rest here for several deep breaths. As you breathe in deeply, say to yourself, "I am content with who I am."

As you breathe out slowly, imagine the subtle stream of breath coming out of the space between your eyebrows. Inhale slowly and deeply again and tell yourself, "I am content with what I have."

Exhale long and slowly and again imagine the breath coming out of the space between your eyebrows. Breathe in deeply again and tell yourself, "What I have accomplished is enough."

As you exhale slowly, imagine the subtle stream of breath coming out the center of the top of your head. With each inhalation, concentrate on feeling contentment fill every part of your body and mind. With each exhalation, let your breath become softer, slower and more subtle.

Continue to rest here as long as you like, allowing a feeling of contentment to expand though every part of you.

When you are ready to come out of this pose, bend your knees and slowly roll to your right side. Inhale as you press your right hand on the floor to help yourself up into a sitting position. Sit with your back against the wall for a few moments to experience the effects of this pose.

Contentment Contemplation

Close your eyes and remember a time when you felt completely happy.

Rest here a few moments to enjoy this feeling of joy. Now, go deeper inside yourself and experience that this joy is always there right inside you.

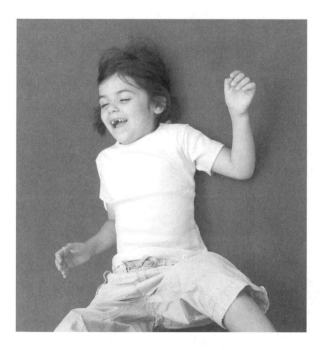

SEVEN

Silence / Stillness

"Like a River, Return to the Source"
Tao Te Ching

In our modern world, silence and stillness have become rare and precious. Children often rush to get dressed and off to school; then, after the demands of their day at school, engage in school activities and return home to television and homework. Restful restorative postures and breathing exercises provide a much-needed opportunity for children to enjoy a few moments of silence and stillness.

Contrary to what you might imagine, most children adore the quiet restful poses. Even very active children, whose concentration span seems short, often prefer restorative poses. Having a few moments of quiet time daily allows them to access their inner strength and wisdom and to restore body and mind.

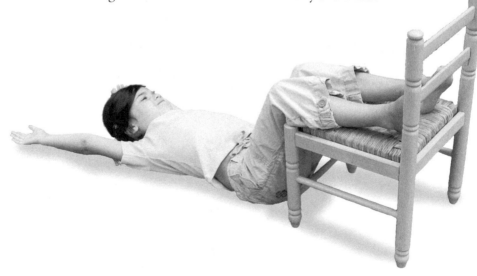

Preparing for Exams

Give students some time before exams to practice restorative poses or breathing exercises. A few minutes of simple movement or breathing exercises will allow them to withdraw their attention from outside distractions, dissolve stress, and be able to better access their innate inner resources.

Blade Squeeze

Inhale and sit up tall in your chair. As you exhale, gently fall forward to rest your forehead on your desk or on a book on your desk. Inhale deeply as you stretch your arms back and interlock your hands on the back of your chair.

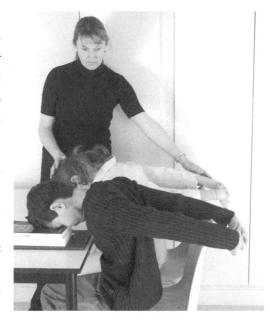

Continue to inhale as you squeeze your shoulders together, gently pulling them back and down. Feel the breath extend your spine. Hold the breath in for a moment and concentrate on your coccyx. Exhale long and slowly, and feel your body and mind begin to relax.

Rest here for three deep breaths. With each inhalation, concentrate on the breath as it lengthens your spine and gently squeeze your shoulders back and down to release any tension in your neck and shoulders. With each exhalation, let your breath be softer, slower and more subtle and feel your body and mind relax more and more.

After each inhalation, hold the breath in for few moments and concentrate on your coccyx. With each exhalation, continue to let your breath become slower and softer. Continue to rest here for a few more breaths, concentrating completely on your breath.

When you are ready to release this pose, exhale as you unclasp your hands, release your arms, and slowly roll up to a seated position. Close your eyes and rest here a few moments, observing your breath and experiencing the effects of this simple yet powerful pose.

Benefits of the *Blade Squeeze*:

This is a simple yet very effective pose that is good to practice anytime to release tension in the upper back and shoulders. Concentrating on the coccyx between each inhalation and exhalation enhances concentration skills, relieves mental tension and creates a calm, centered state.

Touching the Stars

Stand back-to-back with your partner.

As you inhale together, raise your arms to the side and take hold of your partner's hands. Exhaling, gently stretch your arms upward.

Rest here, breathing together for three deep breaths. With each inhalation, feel the breath allowing your body to stretch fully as far as the tips of your fingers and your toes. With each exhalation, stretch your arms up more as if you are touching the sky.

After you have completed three deep breaths, exhale slowly as you lower your arms. Let your arms become lighter and lighter as they slowly float down together. Close your eyes and rest here for a few moments. Continue to concentrate on your breath as you experience the effects of this pose.

Benefits of *Touching the Stars*:

This simple stretch opens the shoulder joints, expands the chest and releases tension in the shoulders and neck.

Clearing the Mind Breathing Technique

Sit up tall in your chair. Inhale and raise your arms, placing your hands on your head with one hand resting on top of the other. Breathe in deeply and feel your spinal column extend. As you exhale slowly, feel yourself growing taller from inside.

Close your eyes and concentrate completely on your breath for three deep breaths. Inhale deeply and feel yourself continue to grow taller. Exhale slowly and feel your shoulders soften as they loosen from side to side. Again, breathe in deeply and feel yourself growing taller from inside. Breathe out slowly and continue to feel yourself growing taller. This time, as you inhale slowly, allow the breath to become softer and more subtle. On the next exhalation, slowly exhale and lower your arms placing your hands on your thighs. Take a moment to feel the effects of this pose. When you are ready, open your eyes.

Benefits of *Clearing the Mind Breathing*:

This breathing exercise opens the spine, clears the mind and is calming and centering for both body and mind. It is an easy way for students to learn how to go beyond distractions and turn their awareness within to discover their inner strength and wisdom.

Brain Stimulating Forward Bend

Stand with your feet in a wide stance. Inhale deeply as you raise your arms upward alongside your ears and press your palms together, feeling your spinal column elongate.

Exhale and bend forward, bringing your elbows toward the floor.

On the next inhalation, shift your torso over to your left side. Exhale slowly as you gently bring your head toward your left knee and place the palms of your hands on the floor on each side of your left foot.

Inhale deeply again as you stretch your torso over to your right side. Exhale slowly as you gently bring your head toward your right knee and place your palms on the floor on each side of your right foot.

On the next inhalation, slowly return your torso back to center position.

Exhale slowly and bend forward, bringing your head toward the floor. As you rest in this position, concentrate on your breath. Feel it release your torso with each exhalation. If your hands touch the floor, you may hold your elbows with your hands. If it is still comfortable for you, continue to hold this position for several deep breaths. With each inhalation, feel the backs of the knees stretch. With each exhalation, surrender more to the subtle breath allowing it to gently release your body more with each exhalation.

When you are ready to release this pose, raise your elbows and bring your palms together as you inhale deeply and slowly return to a standing position, one vertebra at a time. Close your eyes and rest in a standing position for a few moments to experience the effects of this deep forward bend.

Benefits of the *Brain Stimulating Forward Bend*:

This soothing forward bend brings an increased supply of blood and oxygen to the upper body, stimulating the brain.

Three-Part Breath

Sit in a comfortable position. Breathing through your nostrils, observe the breath and allow it to become slower and more subtle with each exhalation.

On the next inhalation, squeeze the muscles in your abdomen gently as you breathe deeply down into your abdomen. Exhaling, squeeze the muscles in your abdomen tighter and feel your abdomen deflate completely. Continue a few more times. Observe the breath streaming out of your nostrils as your abdomen deflates.

Next, as you inhale, first fill your abdomen with breath, then your rib cage. Exhaling, squeeze the muscles of your abdomen and feel your abdomen deflate, then your rib cage.

Again, inhale slowly as you gently squeeze the muscles of your abdomen and feel it expand with breath. Continue to inhale and feel your rib cage and then your chest also expand. Exhale slowly as you squeeze the muscles deep in your abdomen. Continue to exhale long and slowly as you feel your abdomen, then your rib cage, and finally your chest deflate completely. As you practice this deep three-part breathing, observe your breath becoming slower and more subtle. Begin to be aware of the connection between the breath and the mind. Do you feel an increased sense of peace and well-being as the breath becomes slower and more subtle?

Benefits of the *Three-Part Breath*:

The yogic breath expands the breathing capacity and brings an increased supply of oxygen to the lungs, blood, heart, and brain. It also has a beneficial and soothing effect on the nervous system.

Sinking into Silence

"Silence is the energy behind everything we do and all the noise we make in the process."

Herman Melville

We have become so accustomed to constant noise that sometimes complete silence seems almost strange. Yet, in today's busy world, children need quiet time to recharge themselves. Sometimes, in order to experience stillness and silence, over-active children first need to learn how to relax.

Simple stretching exercises, restorative poses and breathing exercises all help children unwind and prepare for a short period of soothing, restorative silence. Learning to enjoy silence will teach students how to access an inner strength and tranquility that will help them succeed in school.

Split Lunge

Come into a lunge position with your left knee bent and your right leg stretched out behind you. Inhale and raise your right arm up alongside your right ear as you look up.

Rest here for three deep breaths. With each inhalation, feel the stretch continue down your right arm, through your torso and all the way into your right leg and foot. With each exhalation, imagine you are sinking deeper and deeper into a calm soothing silence. When you have completed three deep breaths, exhale long and feel your right arm become lighter as it slowly releases back down.

Now, change legs and repeat this deep lunge with your right leg bent in front and your left leg stretched to the back. When you have completed three deep breaths, exhale slowly and feel your left arm become lighter as it floats back down. Close your eyes and rest here for a moment to experience the effects of this deep lunge.

Benefits of the *Split Lunge*:

This deep lunge is soothing to the nervous system. Concentrating on the breath in coordination with each movement calms both body and mind and helps students learn to access their inner resources.

Sinking into Silence

Stand with your feet parallel. Inhale and raise your arms up alongside your ears. Feel your spine elongate.

Exhale and bend your knees a bit as you bend forward, bringing your head toward your knees. Place your palms flat on the floor and rest in this position as you concentrate on the breath for three deep breaths.

85

With each inhalation, feel the stretch in your entire body. With each exhalation, feel your torso release further forward as you imagine yourself sinking deeper and deeper into a sweet silence.

After you have completed three deep breaths, inhale deeply as you slowly roll up one vertebra at a time. Close your eyes and rest here for a few moments to experience the effects of this deep forward bend.

Benefits of *Sinking into Silence*:

This deep forward bend increases blood flow to the brain and soothes the nervous system. It is calming and restorative for both body and mind. It also stretches the hamstring muscles and strengthens the lower back muscles.

The Calm Blue Lake Breathing Technique

Sit back on your heels and form a circle with your friends. Exhale slowly as you fall forward, bringing your hands together in the center of the circle and your forehead to rest on the floor.

Rest here for several deep breaths. With each inhalation, feel the stretch in your entire body. Then, hold the breath in for a moment and concentrate on the space before the exhalation. Imagine a calm blue lake and feel yourself sinking into it. As you exhale slowly, let yourself go deeper and deeper into this calm blue lake.

Continue like this for several deep breaths. After each inhalation, hold the breath in for a moment and feel yourself sinking deeper and deeper into the silence of the calm blue lake between each breath. Rest here as long as you like enjoying this deep silence.

When you are ready to release this pose, inhale and sit back up on your heels. Exhale slowly as you lower your arms. Close your eyes and rest here a few moments to experience the effects of this pose.

Benefits of the *Calm Blue Lake Breathing*:

This simple yet powerful breathing exercise gives a deep rest to both body and mind. It is one of the most effective exercises for learning how to access the source of insight, intuition and creativity. Practicing this pose in a group also creates a feeling of unity and connection.

The Blue Balloon Breathing Technique

Lie on your back with your legs up on a ball or a chair. This exercise may also be done sitting at a desk.

Inhale and begin to blow up your balloon by expanding your chest and rib cage with breath. Imagine you are filling your body with air until it expands completely. As you inhale deeply, visualize the breath going all the way down into your toes, then up your legs. Feel the breath fill your abdomen, rib cage and chest. Then, continue to imagine the breath extending out through your shoulders, arms, hands and up through your neck and head. Hold the breath in for a count of seven and then slowly exhale and observe your balloon deflate.

Repeat this exercise for several deep breaths. With each exhalation, let your breath become slower and more subtle. Experience that the more subtle your breath becomes, the more your body expands with each inhalation.

If you like, you may imagine that you are inflating your balloon with a blue liquid on each inhalation. As you breathe in deeply, see this bright blue color filling your feet, moving up your legs and into your torso and spreading out through your arms and into your hands like blue gloves. Then imagine this deep blue color going up through your neck and into your head. Continue like this for several more deep breaths.

Then rest here for a few extra moments with your eyes closed to experience the effects of this pose.

Benefits of the *Blue Balloon Breathing*:

This inverted position reverses the blood flow, gives a rest to the heart and brings a great renewal of energy. This restorative pose calms and revitalizes all the systems in the body. It releases tension in the back and soothes the nervous system. Taking several minutes every day to rest in this pose is a good way to dissolve fatigue and tension and replenish the calm blue lake that is always there deep inside.

The Sound of Silence Contemplation

Place your attention on the occurrence of a prolonged sound, like that of a bell ringing or a stringed instrument. When the sound stops, hold your attention on the place that the sound occupied. Rest here for several deep breaths. The profound silence of this place will refresh and restore you.

You may ring a small bell at your desk or have students concentrate on the bell or buzzer that signals the beginning or end of a class. You could also use a simple instrument like an auto harp or play a short recording of a stringed instrument.

Benefits of the *Sound of Silence Contemplation:*

This simple technique is an easy way for students to experience an enhanced level of concentration that inspires them to easily sink into a period of silence. This exercise is also effective for enhancing concentration and listening skills.

End the Day Together in Stillness

You and your class may enjoy ending the day together with a few minutes of still-ness. Taking time for a short silent time together at the end of the school day gives students a chance to absorb the material presented during the day. By contemplating their day, students may learn to appreciate and use what they have received.

"Be still. Stillness reveals the secrets of eternity."
Tao Te Ching

Silent Stretch

Sit near the edge of your chair and interlace your fingers behind you with the palms of your hands facing you. Inhaling, breathe in deeply and stretch your interlocked hands toward the back of your chair. Exhaling, lean forward a bit, lift your arms up, and place your palms on the back of your chair with the fingertips facing the seat of the chair. Inhale deeply, expanding your chest and shoulders. Exhaling, relax your shoulders, rolling them back and down away from your ears.

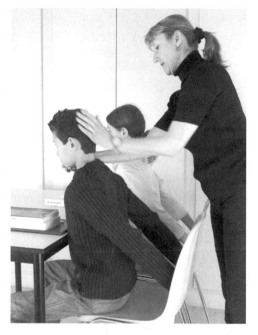

Close your eyes and rest here for three deep breaths. Feel each inhale expand your entire torso. Hold the breath in for a moment and concentrate on the base of your spine. With each exhalation, gently push the palms of your hands against the back of your chair as you release more through your shoulders and neck.

Benefits of the *Silent Stretch:*

This stretch expands the chest, improves posture and releases tension in the shoulders and middle back. It is an easy pose that students may practice at their desk anytime to release tension and take a few moments of silence to recharge and re-center both body and mind.

Standing Dolphin

Stand with your feet in a wide stance. Inhale and stretch your arms up. Bring your elbows near your ears as your fingertips stretch toward the ceiling.

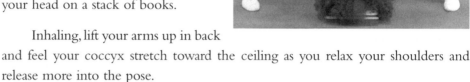

Exhaling, bend forward and place your hands on the floor as you release your head down to rest on the floor. If it is difficult to bring your head to the floor, you may bend your knees or rest your head on a stack of books.

Inhaling, lift your arms up in back and feel your coccyx stretch toward the ceiling as you relax your shoulders and release more into the pose.

Rest here, breathing in deeply and breathing out slowly for three breaths. With each inhalation, feel your entire back stretch. With each exhalation, let your breath become slower and more subtle. Let the exhalation be longer than the inhalation. (For example, breathe in to the count of six and breathe out to the count of nine.) Feel how the long, slow exhalation makes it easier for your body to release more into the pose. After the third long slow exhalation, inhale and return to center. Close your eyes and rest here for a few moments, experiencing the effects of this pose.

Benefits of the *Standing Dolphin*:

The *Standing Dolphin* stretches the backs of the legs and the entire back. It brings an increased supply of blood to the brain and has a relaxing, restorative and calming effect.

Spinal Breath Breathing Technique

Sit in a comfortable position with your spine straight.

Inhale and imagine the breath coming in the center top of your head and flowing all the way down your spine to the base. Hold the breath in for a moment and concentrate on your coccyx. Exhale completely, breathing through the nostrils, and visualize the breath rising up your spine and exiting the top center of your head.

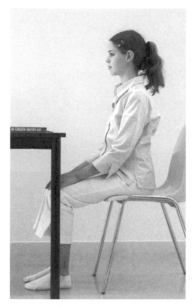

Again, inhale deeply as you visualize the breath coming in the top center of your head and go all the way down the spine. Hold the breath in for a moment and concentrate on the base of your spine. Exhaling, visualize the breath expanding back up through each vertebra, up through your neck and out the top center of your head.

Continue like this for three more deep breaths, observing the breath expanding up and down the channel of your spine. With each exhalation, let your breath become slower and softer.

Benefits of the *Spinal Breath*:

This ancient breathing technique has great power to focus the mind and is one of the easiest and most effective exercises to enhance students' ability to concentrate. It also gives the mind a rest, creates a calm, peaceful feeling and is soothing for the nervous system.

End of the Day Contemplation

Sit back on your heels and bring your forehead to the floor. Place your arms alongside your body with your palms facing the ceiling.

Close your eyes and take a few minutes in silence to remember your day. Observe your day as if it is a movie.

What were your favorite moments of the day? Why?

Recall the moments when you felt the most joy.

What activity was the most fun?

What did you learn today?

What would you like to take home with you to share with others?

If you like, you may share your experience with the class.

What did you discover?

"I realized that some of the most valuable things I learn in school are not always in books."

"I discovered that one of my favorite things about school is my friends."

Benefits of the *End of the Day Contemplation*:

*"Good teachers
+ good students
= Great nation"*
Sai Baba

Developing the habit of taking time to contemplate their day allows students to appreciate what they have received and to discover how they may share their best qualities with others. It also inspires them to develop skills of contemplation and become aware of the personal role they may play in creating a better world.

References and Resources

Books

Deshikachar, TKV. *Reflections on Yoga Sutras of Patanjali.* Chennai, India: Krishnamacharya Yoga Mandiram.

Satyamanda Saraswati, Swami, et al. *Yoga Education for Children: A Manual for Teaching Yoga to Children.* Bihar, India: Bihar School of Yoga, 1985.

Articles

Alexander, Karen. "Yoga at School Poses a Learning Opportunity: Classroom Teachers Note Calming Effect, Better Concentration Among Their Students." *Los Angeles Times,* April 28, 2002.

Briley, John. "A Little Physical Education Goes a Long Way." *The Washington Post,* September 7, 2004.

Brown, Patricia Leigh. "Latest Way to Cut Grade School Stress: Yoga." *The New York Times,* March 24, 2002.

Davies, Gareth A. "Focus on School Sport: Yoga Boosts the Sporting Performance, Says Teacher." *The Daily Telegraph London,* December 30, 1998. Issue PSA-2253.

Falk, Jodi P. "Yoga and Ethics in High School". *The Journal of Dance Education,* Volume 6, Number 4, 2005. Pp. 133-135.

Guthrie, Julie. "Om Schooling: Schools Reach for Yoga to Calm and Collect Students." *San Francisco Chronicle,* February 25, 2002.

Hayes, Ron. "Students Stretch, Bend, Relax with Yoga." *The Palm Beach Post,* May 19, 2002. P. 2C.

Kallinowski, Tess. "School Kids Stretch Away Stress at Yoga." *The Toronto Star,* February 17, 2006.

Kaushik, Y.P., Y. Paul, and M. Gupta. "Yoga for Memory Development of School-going Children." *Yoga Research and Applications: Proceedings of the Fifth International Conference on Frontiers in Yoga Research and Applications.* Bangalore: Vivekananda Kendra Yoga Research Foundation, 2000. Pp. 285-288.

Lynem, Julie N. "Education for the Soul: More Parents Look for Schools to Help Kids Cope with Stress." *San Francisco Chronicle,* October 13, 2000. P. 21.

McCauley, Janie. "Sports Showcase: Schools Dump Dodge-Ball for a New P.E." *Associated Press,* May 30, 2001.

Metz, Barbara F. "Now There's a Fourth R in the Schools: Relaxation." *The Boston Globe,* November 9, 2000.

Morton, Colleen. "Talking Shop with Tony Sanchez." *Yoga Journal,* March/April 2000. P. 26.

Putney, Valerie. "Yoga Can Help Schools: Yoga Instills Discipline." *Greensboro News and Record,* January 17, 1999. Ideas Section.

Singleton, Mark. "Exams the Yoga Way." *Yoga and Health,* May 2004. Pp. 13-15.

Stutkin, Stacie. "Om Schooling: As These Innovative Educators Have Discovered, Assigning Yoga to Kids Can Improve Test Scores and Reduce Disruptive Behavior." *Yoga Journal,* November 2001. Pp. 88-93, 151-153.

_____. "The End of Education is Character." *The Hindu Newspaper,* Chennai, India, November 23, 2005.

Training for Teachers

Teressa Asencia offers special courses, materials and training workshops for teachers.

Email: info@YogaInYourSchool.com

Website: YogaInYourSchool.com

This interactive website is designed to provide a forum for teachers to obtain information, ask questions and share their experiences of teaching Yoga in their schools.